ALWAYS KEEP YOUR HANDS UP

THE SINGLE PREMIUM IMMEDIATE ANNUITY STORY;

KING OF ANNUITIES

"Hail to the King, Baby!"

— Ashley James "Ash" Williams

Gary S Mettler CFP©, CEBS

ISBN: 1499304927
ISBN 13: 9781499304923
Library of Congress Control Number: 2014908274
CreateSpace Independent Publishing Platform
North Charleston, South Carolina

To my two sons,
Scott and Brian
and MaryBeth Kenney

"Do the right thing. It will gratify some people and astonish
the rest."
—Mark Twain

CONTENTS

INTRODUCTION

**"If you can't explain it simply, you
don't understand it well enough."**
—Albert Einstein

Over the last thirty years, being involved in many different facets of the immediate annuity business—and after writing numerous white papers and other articles regarding single premium immediate annuity (SPIA) contracts, the immediate annuity book is due. Over the decades, my high respect for this particular financial product remains unwavering.

Compared to complicated contemporary pretenders to the throne, such as deferred annuities, as we will see in a later chapter, SPIAs are simple and elegant financial products and as we will see in the History chapter have withstood the passing of over a thousand years. Other modern annuity contracts, tracing their design roots to the 1970s, don't even measure as a grain of sand in the hourglass of time when compared the SPIAs's longevity in the marketplace.

In this day in age, its design elegance lies in its simplicity. A simple-promised payment, usually monthly and over the duration of the contract or your life, guaranteed by a life insurance company and requires no consumer management or rocket scientist acumen. Its feel-good quality is expressed time and time again by individuals but only after they become contract owners.

A SPIA is like an old golden retriever who curls by your side next to the fireplace on those long, wintery nights of blowing snow and bitter cold many have come to regard as our current financial climate, its presence is more than welcomed. It's desperately needed.

As a grand financial storm sinisterly rages underneath the radar just outside the front door, people turn to their families, with pencil and paper in hand, gathered at kitchen tables and in dining rooms all around the country desperately trying to cope with personal financial calculations. This has been a persistent and crushing interest rate environment, extending over the last several years with no end in sight. The national one-year bank certificate of deposit rate at .24 percent per year (bankrate.com) is pathetic. Elderly who need income despair and younger individuals fret about safely growing their savings.

But it's not only interest rates. There is also a loss of consumer confidence in the system, a loss stemming from 2002 with the collapse of Enron, WorldCom, Adelphia Communications, and Tyco International destroying thousands of peoples' work lives and retirement hopes. When this is combined with the 2008 financial crisis with the collapse of so many major financial companies that up until 2008 was thought not possible, companies like Lehman Brothers, Bear Sterns, and American International Group (AIG) and this combined with bank bailouts and failure of home ownership all seemingly due to "fat cat" misbehaving and other malfeasance, you create an environment of doubt and fear.

Any safety derived from your perceived job security, health insurance coverage, and retirement financing seems to hang by a very thin thread, indeed. The average person has become tentative, waiting for the other shoe to drop like "children that whistle to ally their tension as they pass a cemetery in the dark."[1]

The grand idea for the "economic fix" is while one segment of the economy is damaged with ultra-low interest rates, another segment gains and enacting more government regulations. Let's only hope the experts are right and in the long run, ultra-low interest rates provide a net benefit to society. Let's not only hope but pray.

But what if you are a member of that damaged segment of society? How do you survive, and what possible steps may you take to not only obtain the safety you long for but the income you desire? Part of the answer lies in a simple, time-tested financial arrangement called a single premium immediate annuity and is the focus of this work.

How will this focus be presented? That's a fair question considering all the previous work, and there is a lot of it regarding the subject of annuities in general. This work will approach the subject matter from what I consider a unique perspective. You won't have to digest any math or at least very little, just an appeal to the "right side" of the brain. The appeal will be intuitive, accomplished by an insightful contract perspective and anecdotes from an industry veteran.

It is also my contention, and as you will see a common theme throughout this book, annuity contracts are purchased or should be purchased for safety purposes (see "Protection" chapter) more than they should be purchased for income purposes. SPIA contracts share a special place in our society because they protect the most fragile elements of society at critical times when they may be under the greatest financial distress. If you get into a personal jam

---

[1] Thomas, Dana L. "The Plungers & the Peacocks, 170 Years of Wall Street" (New York: TEXERE LLC, 2001).

that leads to a real financial jam, the SPIA's property value will soar immensely.

Hopefully, this approach will be consumer friendly, and it will begin to bridge the gap between industry experts, economists, financial writers, and the "ivory tower" crew who highly regard fixed SPIAs based on numerous studies, facts, and figures but find it puzzling why consumers don't share the same respect.

The poet Walt Whitman said, "Wisdom is not finally tested in the schools, Wisdom cannot be pass'd from one having it to another not having it, Wisdom is of the soul, is not susceptible of proof, is its own proof."

Let's see if there is wisdom in my words and not my math.

HISTORY

"To acquire knowledge, one must study; but
to acquire wisdom, one must observe."
—*Marilyn vos Savant*

Introduction

What exactly is an immediate annuity? If you ask different financial advisors, you may receive different answers. Most of the answers will enviably have to do with when the annuity payment is made, which people assume is immediately. For the purpose of this book I use an actuarial definition which means, the timing of the initial payment is inconsequential. It really has to do with when the annuity is "priced." In other words, the annuity is priced immediately when the annuity cost is established by the insurance company and the premium (money) payment is paid for the annuity by the purchaser of the contract. The initial annuity payment from the contract can occur after thirty days, six months, one year, or even several years from the annuity purchase date.

While many individuals will choose to skip this initial chapter, discounting the annuity historical context would be a mistake. Much of the foundation in later chapters is derived from the historical record and some of my conclusions also derive from this record. So, if we are to become not merely knowledgeable but also wise in the way of annuity contracts, how is that accomplished? How can you "observe" annuity contracts? One way of making observations is looking at annuity contracts in their historical contexts and asking questions.

For example, today, since immediate annuity contracts may be purchased from insurance companies that may make payments until you die, we are told it is wise to purchase an immediate annuity, otherwise you might live to very old ages (over ninety) and run out of money. In fact, for many financial advisors, this is the universal and primary reason to purchase one. On the surface, it appears to be a wise use of some of your capital. But, is there historical support for this primary reason to purchase? After all, what was universally true one thousand years ago should be true today.

Ancient Times
I have always struggled with the notion individuals primarily purchase immediate annuities because they were afraid they were going to live too long and die penniless. Immediate annuity contracts have been around at least as long as the Roman times. There is even speculation they existed in ancient Babylonian 2,500 BC and Egypt. You also find annuities being purchased and sold in Europe during and after the medieval ages. The average person back in those days just didn't live too long. But annuities were popular. If the average person back then didn't live too long, why would they be popular? What was going on?

Petty city and state wars constantly ebbed and flowed across medieval Europe. The Black Death from about 1347 to 1351 killed off an entire third of the European population, or about twenty-five million people. The English and French Hundred Year War raged from 1337 to 1453 and peasant revolts were numerous and ruthlessly suppressed. The food supply was constantly threatened by crop failures due to unanticipated climate changes. In metropolitan areas, access to clean water was problematic. Natural disasters, earthquakes, floods and tsunamis in the Mediterranean Sea caused entire populations to relocate and suffer death and starvation. Political events and the environment posed all kinds of risks to one's longevity.

Property, for the most part, consisted of land, goods, livestock and coinage not easily transported around the countryside if you had to leave town real fast. But then there was this thing called an annuity. A piece of paper you could just easily roll up, place in your tunic, and skip town for a while, just a simple promise by the king or queen to pay some future income if you lived. How convenient was that?

A mutual aid society for the Legions of Rome granted an annuity to a retired legionnaire at age forty-six that would pay for an estimated fourteen years (life expectancy). A written table (Table of Ulpian), for the purpose of estimating expected lifetime annuity payments, appears to have been established sometime around 40 BC to about 225 AD. According to this table, you make it to about age sixty. If you are age sixty or older you get another five years.

After the collapse of Rome and its money economy, the world entered into a "goods economy," and only in the very Northern reaches of Italy did money, for the most part, maintain value. It was only toward the end of the Middle Ages when trade and commerce started to once again flourish money (gold/silver) became center stage for com-mercial financing purposes. The Catholic Church had edicts opposing excessive interest (usury) charged to individuals, as up until that time, loans were primarily used for con-sumption purposes and not backed by collateral.

In order to finance wars and municipal pursuits, Genoa, Florence, and Venice issued loans in the form of annuities against their "credit." In 1470 Genoa had outstanding obligations of eleven million lira that increased to forty-seven million lira by 1597.

In the geographical areas of Flanders and Brabant, what is now mostly Belgium, the ancient city of Tourani boasts archives containing annuity certificates issued to individuals in 1229. In 1265, one Robert Norman of Utrecht purchased a survivorship annuity with his son for four hundred Parisian livres. The contract actually contained a purchasing power clause in the case the Parisian livres declined relative to the Tournaise sous (another currency of the time).

In 1549, Count William of Julich applied for an annuity from the city of Ghent not only on himself but "for all his towns and villages and for his lands and people." As early as 1449, town officials would establish an annuity office and post its location in an announcement placed on the church door telling annuitants where to call for their money. How safe was that? A person had to actually appear prior to collecting any money. Only the annuitant could benefit from this arrangement.

It appears both Robert Norman and Count William had other reasons to purchase an annuity than just their own immediate financial concerns.

The idea of mortality issues and annuities took a giant step forward when Lorenzo Tonti made a proposal to Cardinal Mazarin to help revive French finances toward the end of the seventeenth century. Lorenzo proposed to raise a sum of 25,000,000 livres in exchange for an annual "average" interest rate of 4.10 percent or 1,025,000 livres to be divided into ten classes of individuals by age range with each class receiving 102,500 livres. Nine groups had age ranges of seven consecutive years with the age sixty-three and older crowd being treated as the tenth class. Younger class members paid more to get into the fund and accepted lower interest rates compared to older class members who paid less to get into the fund and received higher interest rates.

Each class was closed and the pool formed. Survivors received a prorate share, distributed annually, of the 102,500 livres allocated to their class. When the last class member died, interest payments were discontinued and the fund securing the interest payments for this particular class reverted to the French crown.

Ultimately the proposal was rejected and when Lorenzo attempted to press the issue by authoring and then circulating a politically charged pamphlet about his scheme in 1669, the French Minister of Finance had him tossed in the Bastille. It's thought Lorenzo died around 1695 in prison, poor and forgotten.

However, as with all ideas of any substance, they rarely die with their creators. Lorenzo's annuity scheme, now referred to as a Tontine, took root. In 1670, just one year after the publication of Lorenzo's pamphlet, the Dutch city of Kampen issued a Tontine of 100,000 florins in 400 individual certificates of 250 florins each. A single "investor," Jacob Van Dael, purchased the entre deal! He distributed a pamphlet, or what we might call a prospectus today, outlining how his original 400 investors, based on their survival, would collect on the annuity. How sad there was no mention of Lorenzo.

At this time and for the next few centuries the concept of mortality (how long individuals may be expected to survive) intertwined with the concept of compound interest (interest that itself earns interest from year to year) developed. A series of mathematicians: John De Witt, John

Hudd, Edmund Halley, James Dodson, Abraham DeMoivre, Thomas Simpson, and many others advanced what we call today actuarial science.

In one of my favorite early annuity schemes that should serve as one of the earliest warnings to investors in this day and age is to beware of credit substitution or offered changes in terms and conditions by the issuer (insurance company) after the annuity contract is issued.

It so happened in 1720 that English crown finances were at a low point, plagued by debt. In addition, life annuities granted by the crown at the close of the seventeenth century were in significant payment arrears. Annuity bargains purchased by individuals were in danger of default. However, an ingenious idea arose and the King, along with his governors, wanted out of the annuity obligations. Also at the time there existed the South Sea Company, a joint-stock company that was created as a kind of public-private partnership with the goal of reducing public debt. The company was granted a monopoly to trade with South America, but this geographic area of the world was controlled by a divided Spain embroiled in the War of Spanish Succession. The price of stock in the South Sea Company rose and ebbed in spectacular fashions, and due to the stocks' great popularity, the crown sought to offer South Sea Company stock to annuitants in exchange for the crown's annuity obligations.

The crown initially offered to purchase from short term annuitants eleven-and-a-half years of future annuity payments by exchanging their payments for South Sea Company stock with additional South Sea Company stock to cover payment arrearages. This offer was quickly taken up by stressing annuitants. Other classes of annuitants were made similar offers, and they were also snapped up just as quickly. In this fashion, it was recorded that 666,821 British pounds per year were saved by the crown as the annuity obligations were traded in by their owners for South Sea Company Stock.

In January of 1720, the Stock was traded at 128 British pounds and by the end of May it had reached 550 pounds. In a "speculating frenzy" the stock price had climbed to 1,000 pounds by early August before collapsing. Needless to say entire annuitant classes were bankrupt and the whole British economy suffered for years after the South Sea Company's collapse.

The American Experience
What about the American experience? When it came to annuities, certainly America benefited from the European and Middle East experience.

On January 11, 1759, the Presbyterian Minister Fund was founded in Philadelphia, Pennsylvania. The original goal of this organization was to provide financial support to poor and distressed Presbyterian Ministers, their widows and orphans. In 1845, this organization started providing annuity contracts to its members. Eventually, the Presbyterian Annuity Company was created and continued to issue annuity contracts well past 1875.

In 1792, the Universal Tontine was created in Philadelphia with the idea of transacting annuity business in all the federal states. From this tontine developed the Insurance Company of North America.

At the close of the eighteenth century, annuity transactions were almost entirely taken over by the fledging life insurance industry that benefited from all the previous centuries' leaps in actuarial science. Insurance supervision was established by the states around 1799. Also in 1812, in

Philadelphia, the Pennsylvania Company for Insurance on Lives and Granting Annuities was founded.

As the twentieth century dawned, the family unit started to change. Extended families that provided some de facto annuity financial support dwindled and the numbers of multigenerational family households diminished. Older people were just starting to become more independent.

Data compiled by the Temporary National Economic Commission (TNEC) in 1941 indicated up until the 1800s, specifically from about 1866 to 1920, premiums (US dollars) from life insurance transactions dominated the life insurance industry while annuity premium averaged only a paltry 1.50 percent of the total life insurance premium totals.

However, this was all set to change with the onset of the Great Depression and associated financial panics. The floodgates were open and annuity premium came rushing into life insurance company coffers—obviously due to the public's fear of going broke and not for fear of living too long and running out of money. No one just woke up one day during the 1930s and rushed out to see his or her friendly local insurance agent to purchase an annuity because that person was afraid he or she was going to live too long and run out of money at age eighty-five or ninety. Banks were failing left and right. There was a real fear of going broke immediately. The primary purchase reason was safety (not going broke), what was happening then at the moment and not what might happen thirty years from then (longevity).

The TENC reported 68 percent of all annuity premiums received by the life insurance industry (twenty-six large life insurance companies) during the years 1913 and 1937 were received between 1933 and 1937. From 1934 through 1936, the premium from new annuity transactions actually exceeded the premium from new life insurance transactions for the twenty-six large life insurance companies in the TENC study. By 1938, life insurance company annuity reserves (assets insurance companies are required to keep) totaled $2.67 billion while life insurance reserves were $16.83 billion.

However, what is still remembered today, particularly by state regulators, is the tremendous financial loss suffered by the life insurance industry due to the annuity contracts placed in the 1930s. Up until that time, having very little practical annuity experience relative to their tremendous life insurance experience, and on the now massive scale being required of the industry by consumers purchasing annuity contracts, the insurance industry completely misjudged their annuity pricing. As we will see, this mistake repeats itself in subsequent decades.

Life insurance industry earnings declined over two decades; this was primarily due to the poor profitability of annuity contracts. The first factor attributable to this profitability decline was the general fall in interest rates. Insurance companies were not able to invest their assets appropriately to service annuity payment liabilities over their long payment durations. The second factor was the life insurance industry misjudged how long annuitants would survive. Earlier in the 1930s, the life insurance industry used a mortality table called the 1868 American Experience Table for Mortality. This table was sixty-two years old and was created just after the conclusion of the US Civil War. It made no distinction between males or females and listed individuals age seventy as having a life expectancy of 8.49 years. However, a newer table created in 1938 indicated female life expectancy at 15.62 years. But by this time it was too late for all the annuities issued prior to 1938. Mortality and interest will be discussed in the chapter on contracts.

These annuities were very much like the SPIAs we know and love today. There was either immediate income or deferred income contracts. Some contracts were purchased with single payments while others were purchased by making a series of payments. Depending on the contract, consumers could set payment structures in advance, elect payment structures, or surrender their contracts for cash.

In the 1940s, 1950s, and 1960s, annuity development primarily happened in the group annuity markets. Insurance companies offered group annuity contracts to large employers for the benefit of their many employee and the rise of the defined benefit pension plan (an annuity offered by an employer) occurred.

Also starting around the 1920s, there was, to a limited extent, individual immediate annuities distributed by the organized charities as a way to raise money for their causes. The American Council on Gift Annuities was created in 1927 to promote philanthropy by helping charities raise money by providing uniform practices and annuity pricing. In this case, the charity issues a Charitable Gift Annuity (CGA), and upon the annuitant(s) death, the annuity payments cease and the residual annuity value goes to the charity. Today, you will find charities such as the American Red Cross, Salvation Army, UNICEF, and many others transacting in both immediate income and deferred income contracts.

The Federal Government provides tax incentives to purchase CGAs that are over and above tax incentives to purchase commercial annuity contracts from life insurance carriers (see the "Tax Implications" chapter).

Structured Settlement markets incorporating immediate income and deferred income contracts evolved starting in the 1980s. These transactions involve a defendant who pays for an annuity contract, usually held by a third party for the benefit of an injured person, the plaintiff, who is the annuitant. The idea is to settle a judgment or reach a settlement with the plaintiff that is tax favored and that permits each party, defendant and plaintiff, to achieve favorable benefits. The defendant may achieve a favorable settlement cost and the removal of their liability. The plaintiff receives the safety of the annuity, tax free income, and the ability to begin to put the settlement in their past. Books have been written on these annuities, but at this point, for our purposes, a mere mention will suffice.

Deferred annuities, while not discussed at any length in this book except as how they relate to immediate annuities, are immensely popular today. Annuity owners actively manage deferred annuity contracts' cash values and might access these cash values by making cash withdrawals. These kinds of contracts didn't really exist until the late 1970s. We will see how the tide turned for deferred annuity contracts more in depth later in the "Pretenders to the Throne" chapter.

I often cite a hypothetical conversation to make a satirical point about how important longevity aspects of SPIAs are when the scope of their historical relevance is reviewed. The rhetorical question is as follows: Is it really possible ancient Romans and medieval Europeans purchased lifetime annuities because they were afraid they were going to live too long and run out of money? I can just hear their conversations now:

Tiberius: Hey, Brutus.

Brutus: Yes, Tiberius?

Tiberius: You know, Brutus, you are now age twenty, and the latest rage at the forum these days are lifetime annuities that protect you from longevity risk.

Brutus: You think I should be concerned?

Tiberius: Absolutely, Brutus! What are you going to do if you actually make it to age twenty-five and run out of money?

At this point, I think it is pretty clear individuals, historically, purchased immediate annuity contracts for a host of reasons that don't have much to do with lifetime income. I believe individuals recognize their lives can be altered for the worse in an instant of time (see anecdotes). Like other forms of insurance, in order to protect at least a part of their assets, individuals historically turned to the immediate annuity markets to provide protection. Nothing has really changed, which is why these same reasons exist today.

So, if safety then becomes the first reason to purchase an immediate annuity, what is the second reason? As we will see, later on, it has a lot to do with income taxes.

Chapter Summary

• An immediate annuity's payment is usually monthly income for the contract purchaser guaranteed by the insurance company at the annuity purchase date; it can be paid at any future date. The initial income date, depending on the contract, can be thirty days or deferred as long as thirty years from the purchase date.

• Early European and even older historical records clearly show individuals purchased single-premium immediate annuity contracts (SPIAs) for safety reasons.

• Beginning in the 1930s, Americans rushed to purchase SIPA contracts from commercial insurance companies because banks and financial markets were failing, and they wanted safe financial institutions in which to place their savings.

• Charities offer their own SPIA contracts, and the structured settlement annuity industry uses SPIAs to settle litigation matters. Both industries offer SPIA contracts featuring current income payments and deferred income payments.

End Notes
Kopf, Edwin W. "The Early History of the Annuity." *The Educational Committee of the Society of Actuaries*, (1927). Paper presented on the Fundamentals of Insurance.

Poterba, James M. "The History of Annuities in the United States." NBR Working Paper Series. Working Paper 6001. *National Bureau of Economic Research,* (April 1997).

THE CONTRACT

"Louise, people in this country aren't interested
in details. They don't even trust details.
The only thing they trust is headlines."
—*Senator Kevin Keeley (Gene Hackman)*
from The Birdcage, 1996

Introduction
It constantly surprises me consumers don't fully cherish the
fact they actually receive a real live contract when they purchase a SPIA. The fact the purchase transaction involves
an actual contract is a huge reason to even make the
purchase in the first place. After all, no one gets a contract
when they purchase a mutual fund, a securities brokerage
account, a stock, a bond, a bank savings account, or even
a United States Government savings bond!

Interpretation
How things are written is very important, but more important is the interpretation of the written word. It's really
important people understand what they read. This is where
the agent can help out.

I often recite a story about interpretation based off an
old Eek and Meek carton by Howie Schneider. In this story
there is Dennis and Mr. Wilson. Dennis is this kind of ne're-
do-well kid who always manages to come up smelling like
a rose. While Mr. Wilson has his number, Dennis always

manages to get the better of him. One very sunny and hot day, Dennis opens a lemonade stand on his front lawn with this huge hand-painted sign that reads: "All You Can Drink for a Dime." Mr. Wilson says to himself, *Now, I got him; I'll just teach him a little lesson.* Mr. Wilson strolls over to Dennis's yard and orders a glass of lemonade and forks over a dime. Dennis carefully pours a tiny bit from a huge jug of lemonade into this really small Dixie cup and hands it to Mr. Wilson. "Here you go Mr. Wilson," Dennis says with a smiling face.

After seeing the Dixie cup, Mr. Wilson quietly chuckles to himself and smirks. "All you can drink for a dime, indeed," and quickly downs the cup's contents. Mr. Wilson immediately puts his cup down on the stand and tells Dennis to "fill 'er up". Dennis once again takes out his lemonade jug and slowly refills Mr. Wilson's Dixie cup. But before Mr. Wilson can down it, Dennis blurts out, "That will be a dime, Mr. Wilson."

Mr. Wilson smugly points to the sign and says, "Dennis, your sign says, 'All You Can Drink for a Dime.'" Dennis looks at Mr. Wilson and then at the sign, and then at Mr. Wilson again, and says innocently, "Why, Mr. Wilson, that is all you can drink for a dime."

General

I'm astonished by how many consumers, years after making an annuity contract purchase, cannot find their contract. Out the gate, the best piece of general advice I can give about annuities to any annuity consumer is *don't lose your contract.* But, if the contract is lost, a consumer or his or her agent needs only to phone the carrier and complete a lost policy or contract form to receive a replacement copy. Because of constant changes in the annuity industry, the contract you purchased even five years ago is probably not the same contract the company is selling today.

The next best piece of advice I can give to a consumer is *read your contract*. The contract represents your property, and chances are you paid a lot of money for it. The best time to do this is when the agent delivers the contract to you after your purchase date. Make the agent sit down with you to go over the contract. The old custom is for the agent to obtain a "delivery receipt" when they give you the contract. An annuity contract delivery receipt is signed and dated by you, claiming you received the property.

As an agent, I used to bring a second copy of the contract that could be marked up as I reviewed each section with the purchasing consumer. This marked up copy resided in my file as support of the contract delivery review. In today's day and age, much of this contract delivery process is lost. Most annuity agents today prefer to just mail the contract to the consumer and don't bother with setting aside meeting time to obtain a delivery receipt.

However, from a consumer prospective, this is the best opportunity you have to sit with the agent to discuss the contract. If the agent can't address all your concerns then, you have an opportunity to speak with a home office representative to help clear up matters. If you are not satisfied with the answers you receive, and because of provisions in your contract, this is also you best opportunity, if you are not happy, to seek a full refund of your money. The annuity agents and carriers know this, so if you press them for an actual meeting date and time, they will feel compelled to comply. Don't feel uncomfortable involving others such as other financial professionals, CPAs, attorneys, and even competent family members in the annuity contract delivery/acceptance process. If there is a mistake or a misunderstanding, it's in the consumer's absolute best interest to catch it at the contract delivery date.

As an agent working with a consumer, I was trained to respect the value of the property. It is valuable property indeed, not only for its potential cash value, but because the contract explains all the guarantees and terms and conditions. It serves as a consumer defense. If the agent recommends a replacement transaction (a transaction where one annuity contract is proposed to replace an existing annuity contract or life insurance policy), and something goes terribly wrong with the replacement transaction that isn't discovered until many months or even years later following the transaction, the replacing agent and carrier can't feint ignorance about the replaced contract or policy if the consumer gave them his or her existing contract or policy.

Regarding a replacement transaction, the consumer should always give their existing annuity contract or life insurance policy to the replacing agent. Make them take it, and after they take it, make the replacing agent give you a receipt for your property.

Once the original contract is in the replacing agent's hands and it goes to the replacing carrier, it is subject to the annuity purchase suitability review process as disclosed information required by the states. The carrier should review the replaced contract along with all the other information collected in the replacement process to determine if the proposed annuity purchase transaction is in the consumer's best economic interest.

A good agent is trained to review the replaced annuity contract or life insurance policy prior to taking an application for a new annuity contract, and then collect the contract or policy from the consumer, give the consumer a receipt for the contract or property, and then send the replaced contract or policy along with all the other paperwork to the replacing carrier's home office. The replacing carrier contacts the replaced carrier to facilitate a direct transfer of the cash value of the replaced contract or policy. Part of this procedure is sending the replaced contract or policy back to the carrier that issued it. Once the funds are received by the replacing carrier, the new annuity contract is issued and delivered to the consumer.

However, as can be expected, shortcuts are available as agents and home offices don't really want to get into all the paper shuffling associated with older annuity contracts or life insurance policies. Transaction costs escalate. In order to create less hassle for the agent and the replacing carrier and reduce transaction costs, replacement forms agents are required to complete have provisions (small print) to claim the replaced contract was "lost or destroyed." The consumer must sign this form. If the consumer signs this form, the replacing agent and their carrier are relieved of the responsibility of collecting the replaced contract, and the transaction time is speeded up.

After all, if the consumer didn't have a copy of his or her contract or policy to give to the replacing agent because it was lost or destroyed, it might take that consumer three to four weeks or longer to actually receive a duplicate contract or policy from his or her existing carrier. Replacing agents and their carriers really don't want to wait for the consumer to receive duplicates, as it slows transaction activity to a crawl. This gives consumers additional time to consider their replacement decisions.

Before we get into SPIA contract components, let's look at a little contract law relative to SPIAs and what makes SPIA contracts so special.

Business is primarily conducted through the use of contracts. There are tons of books written about contract law. So I won't go into any great depth here. But, contracts are normally written agreements that are enforceable in courts of law. There are three basic tenets that create a contract. There is an offer, an acceptance via an "arms-length negotiation," and consideration (money) is paid. Arms-length negotiation means the parties bargain back and forth with equal or near equal bargaining power until they can reach an agreement.

However, SPIA contract consumers can't bargain back and forth with the SPIA carrier; there is no bargaining that affects pricing or specific SPIA contract terms and conditions. SPIA contracts are strictly a "take it or leave it" proposition from the carrier issuing the contract.

Because the SPIA consumer has no bargaining power, this kind of contract is called an "adhesive" contract, and in general, adhesive contracts are inherently unfair agreements for the consumer. However, to facility business activity, standardized contracts permit insurance companies to quickly issue contracts to consumers who, as a group, all receive the same terms, conditions, and pricing, and then have to decide on the merits of any one SPIA contract in exchange for the their money aka premium cost.

The key word here is "standardized." Who sets the standard in order to protect the disadvantaged consumer? What powerful consumer ally exists that keeps the insurance carriers in line, causing knees to quake in carrier home offices across the country? The fifty different state insurance departments, that's who. Very few financial entities have fifty different state regulator organizations in addition to the Federal Government breathing down their necks.

The insurance carriers are required to file a copy of the SPIA contract aka "form" with each state they are seeking approval to sell that specific contract via their agents to residents of the state. If the state has a problem with the contract's design, organization, language, look, feel, readability, pricing, or even type font size, the carrier will need to file and keep filing until the carrier gets it right.

If there is a contract mistake or something is not clear or even omitted and it damages the SPIA consumer or even merely places the SPIA consumer in a bad position, and upon an investigation, the state has the last word and will invariably find in favor of the consumer. In this manner, the state primarily protects the consumer because the carrier had their chance when filing the "standardized" contract seeking state sale approval.

In the annuity product development phase, I sat, hour upon hour, in endless meetings in conference rooms of fifteen to twenty midlevel insurance company departmental mangers, painstakingly reading the difficult language of annuity contracts line by line just to make sure we got it right prior to filing the contract form with each state. Because each state is different, you might have to consider variations of the same contract just to meet the separate guidelines of any particular state.

In all cases, the state steps in for the consumer to level the playing field. This is a state provided protection and another good reason to purchase a SPIA contract because you have a big brother looking out for you. State insurance departments are there primarily to protect consumers, and every state has one. Because of state consumer protections, another good consumer tip is to *always purchase a SPIA contract approved by your resident state.* In other words, if you are a resident of New York State, make sure the SPIA contract you purchase is approved by New York State for sale to New York residents.

Make sure to have the agent verify if the SPIA contract he or she is representing has the proper state approval. If you are not convinced you can contact the home office and make the necessary inquiry. Don't be tempted to purchase another carriers' contract in a nonresident state just because you happen to work there or happen to be there visiting family where the agent takes the application. Generally, this transaction is permissible, if also the contract is delivered to you at the location where you purchased it, but you may be giving up important resident state protections by entering into this type of transaction (see "Protection" chapter).

One of the biggest consumer complaints is the readability of the contract itself. The language is just, well, so legal. The terms are unfamiliar to the average consumer and sometimes the practical impact of the contract terms may be lost on the average consumer. This is one reason consumers should compel their agents to review contracts with them.

In order to foster a better understanding, sometimes carriers develop supporting disclosures and colorful marketing materials that may or may not also be subject to state department of insurance reviews. But none supersede the contract itself, so these additional disclosures should not entirely be relied upon. If consumers ask agents to produce a "specimen" (sample) contract, the agent can deliver and review it with a consumer prior to making an application and purchase. Certified Public Accountants (CPAs) and or attorneys, working with their consumer clients, are more likely to request these specimen contracts in advance of making an application.

Parties

Let's look at the parties to a SPIA contract.

The carrier is the life insurance company that receives the annuity premium from the consumer, issues the SPIA contract, guarantees and makes the SPIA payments, and upon the owner's request, provides administrative services.

The Owner controls the property and is an individual or even an entity, if the contract permits entity ownership. The owner can direct payments, change beneficiaries and payees, and exercise contract options. The owner also has property disposition rights such as ownership changes and pledging the contract for a loan. The owner pays the income taxes on the annual taxable income the SPIA produces. There can be a single owner or even joint individual owners. Joint owners are usually spouses, but if the contract permits, they maybe nonspouses. Joint owners must unanimously agree, in writing, to exercise ownership rights.

The Contingent Owner is the person who takes over upon the death of the owner and can exercise contract ownership rights. Some SPIA contracts don't permit contingent owners. These contracts automatically transfer contract ownership to the annuitant or beneficiary if an owner who is not also the annuitant dies. Automatic successive ownership can be problematic if consumers don't understand how the succession works (see chapter examples). However, carriers created automatic succession because consumers either failed to nominate contingent owners or contingent owners died and a new successor was never named, so SPIA contracts had a nasty habit of falling into the owner's estate when the owner died, where they are subject to the probate process.

Remember SPIAs are permanent, irrevocable contracts and how the property transfers from one person to another is controlled by the contract. You can't just conveniently liquidate SPIAs to cash if the property transfers don't go according to your designs.

The Annuitant is the person or persons (maximum of two people) who determine the life expectancy (measuring life) of any life-contingent annuity payment. When the annuitant(s) dies, the contract payment, if based on the annuitant(s) life, terminates. Or, depending on the type of payment, if it's a "period-certain" payment (legacy portion), it goes to the contract beneficiary(s). This is also called the "death benefit." The annuitant(s) may not be changed once the contract is issued by the carrier.

The Payee, nominated by the owner, is a person or entity nominated by the owner. If permitted by the contract to receive the annuity payment, usually the payee is the owner. If the contract permits, the owner may elect several payees with each payee receiving an equal or unequal portion of the payment. The payee(s) and the payee's share of the payment may also be changed by the owner(s) after the contract is issued.

The Beneficiary(s), nominated by the owner, is the person or persons who receive the remaining payments or value of the remaining payments (death benefit) of the SPIA contract when the annuitant dies. There can be more than one beneficiary, and beneficiaries may share equally or unequally in the death benefit. Beneficiaries or their percentage benefit may be changed by the owner after the contract is issued by the carrier. The beneficiary may also be irrevocably named by the owner. If irrevocably named, the beneficiary may not be changed unilaterally by the contract owner. In addition, all contract ownership rights are subject to the written approval of the irrevocable beneficiary. Naming an irrevocable contract beneficiary is a powerful property control option, and while there could be very good reasons for the owner to name an irrevocable beneficiary, it should not be done lightly.

The Contingent Beneficiary(s), nominated by the owner, is the person who will receive the remaining payments or value of the remaining payments (death benefit) of the SPIA contract, who also happens to survive the beneficiary, when the annuitant dies. Some owners forget to name a new beneficiary after the beneficiary dies. In this case, the contingent beneficiary will inherit the SPIA contract. There can be more than one contingent beneficiary and they can share equally or unequally in the death benefit. Contingent beneficiaries can be changed by the contract owner after the contract issue date if no irrevocable beneficiary is also named. If there is an irrevocable beneficiary, the owner will need to get the written permission of the irrevocable beneficiary to change the contingent beneficiary.

[Note: There are advanced specialty beneficiary designations that, for example, pay SPIA death benefits to children of the beneficiary(s) if the beneficiary is not alive at the death of the annuitant. In this case, it isn't necessary to name the children—in fact they might not even exist because they are not born yet.]

The Agent is the licensed individual who takes the initial application, collects the annuity premium, and delivers the contract to the consumer and provides consumer servicing support after the contract is issued. Typically, after the contract is issued by the carrier, the agent remains as the servicing agent unless removed by the owner.

Provisions

Let's look at some SPIA contract provisions and what they mean.

Free Look: This provision is located on the cover page of the contract. It is the period of time previously discussed the owner has to review the contract with the agent. The free look period doesn't begin until the owner actually receives the contract. So, if the contract can't get delivered for three weeks because the owner is out of the country on vacation, then the free look period will not begin until the owner returns and he or she can get his or her hands on the contract. The duration of the free look period can be anywhere from ten to sixty days, depending on the contract and the transaction type and the regulating state.

Typically "cash" transactions have shorter free look periods than "replacement" transactions. A replacement transaction is where a consumer "exchanges" an existing deferred annuity contract or life insurance policy for the SPIA contract. Because a replacement transaction entails the consumer surrendering his or her previous annuity contract or life insurance policy, some states make sure there is sufficient time for the consumer to consider the transaction. In New York, replacement transactions have sixty-day free look periods, the longest of any state. If a replacement transaction annuity is free looked, then the former carrier has to stand ready to reinstate your former annuity contract or life insurance policy, depending on the case.

If the owner received a payment or two and elects to exercise his or her free look right by sending the contract back to the carrier for a premium refund, typically the carrier will return his or her premium less annuity payments received. Technically the contract never existed.

Once the free look period lapses, traditional SPIAs are irrevocable contracts. You will not be able to receive a full or even a partial refund of your premium without some serious legal intervention. This could take years, and there is no guarantee of success. However, in many cases, irrevocable contracts can be a good thing; they help consumers protect their money and their legacy wishes many years after the SPIA contract is issued by the carrier (see "Protection" chapter).

The declarations page: This is the page that appears in order after the cover page. It contains pertinent information relative to the SPIA contract and the contract number. The owner(s) and annuitant(s) are listed along with their ages, the premium payment amount, and the contract date or "purchase date." Beneficiaries might also be listed here. This page also contains a description of the annuity payment (see "Variability" chapter) and the initial payment date. The declarations page might also indicate if the SPIA is an individual retirement arrangement (IRA).

The declarations page should be the focus of the free look review. Is the information correct? Is the initial payment date, payment frequency, and the payment amount what you wanted? Are the age(s) correct? Are the names spelled correctly? Is it really an IRA or was there a mistake made and the carrier issued the SPIA contract as a non-IRA. The free look period is your best time to make corrections. Any mistakes can affect your income, claims, and income taxation.

Owners' Rights: This is a very important section. Who can be an owner and what an owner can do may determine if you want to even purchase the particular contract in the first place. If the owner has no right to change ownership, then this severely hampers his or her property disposition rights. For example, you may have purchased the SPIA contract as an individual, and then years later created a living trust to hold title to all your property. If the SPIA prohibits you from changing ownership, you will not be able to place the SPIA in your living trust. If your will states your children are to receive SPIA contracts at your death, the estate administrator will not be able to purchase SPIA contracts in the estate's name as owner, and then transfer ownership to your kids. If you just want to make a gift of your contracts while you are still alive by changing owner-ship of your contracts to your favorite charity or even your adult children or siblings, you will not be able to do so. *Generally, I would avoid SPIA contracts that don't confer the right of the owner to change ownership.*

Death of whom and when death occurs: I find this the most frustrating of all SPIA provisions because individuals can be owners and or annuitants and owners or annuitants don't necessarily have to be the same person. Because owner and or annuitant death may occur before the initial payment date or after the initial payment date, and because the initial payment date can be several months or years away, the contract may call for different death benefit treatments, depending on who dies when. What happens when who dies when? It kind of sounds like the beginning of the old Abbot and Costello routine of; "who's on first." It depends on your contract.

Not knowing what happens to the contract when the various parties die can be disastrous. A very attractive fea-ture of the SPIA, a substitute for a last will and testament, is it avoids the probate process. The probate process is a very public administration via a probate court and a probate judge of a deceased person's estate which is comprised of existing assets and liabilities at their death.   In this process a persons' last will and testament, a legal document, directs the probate court how to settle one's affairs. If the con-sumer has no valid will at death, there are state imposed rules that vary from state to state that dictate what happens to your assets and liabilities and who gets what (if anything). SPIAs prevent untidy public disclosures that may accompany the probate process by making death benefit payments directly to contract beneficiaries. Therefore, no wills, courts or judges are needed. One reason why consumers purchase SPIAs is they want certain things to happen right away and they don't necessarily want the whole world to know about. Take the following two real life examples.

Older Man Second Marriage
An older man in his second marriage purchases a SPIA with "his money" in order to receive income. He wants to call all the "shots" so he is the sole owner. He names his new, much younger wife as the annuitant. He wants the payment over her life expectancy, as he intends for the contract to revert to her upon his death and wants the payment paid over her life. But just in case she dies first, he names himself the beneficiary to receive the legacy portion of the SPIA, if any, at her death. His kids from his first marriage, who love their mother, don't care much for his new wife. They will inherit the rest of his estate through his will. Regardless, he doesn't really want his kids to know about the SPIA contract purchase intended for his new wife. Sounds like a good plan right? Several years later, as expected, he dies, predeceasing his new wife. What happened?

The SPIA contract per the contract language reverts to the joint owner, but there wasn't one because he was the sole owner and wanted the sole control "to call all the shots." The next in line per the SPIA contract language to own would have been the beneficiary, but because the owner and beneficiary was the same person, this couldn't happen either. The contract happened to be silent regarding successive ownership control after this time, so the property reverted to his estate and his adult kids got it via the probate process! The kids became the new owners of the contract intended for his new wife. She was immediately disinherited. Not cool.

I asked the attorney why the parties, knowing the vast difference in age, in this case twenty years, purchased such a contract? The attorney said it was the best priced 30-years period certain and lifetime thereafter SPIA at the time.

Frankly, this is the kind of result consumers, who don't work with knowledgeable annuity agents about the contracts they represent, can expect. It's tempting for consumers and some agents to just look at these products from a price only perspective without really knowing how the contract works, treating them as some type of commodity. In the end, you can really pay for such a myopic perspective. If you think it's expensive dealing with a professional annuity agent, wait until you see the cost of dealing with an amateur.

Obliviously, this was not a good SPIA contract form for this particular client. There are better SPIA forms for this particular purpose (see "Brokerage" chapter).

Older Father Adult Son
An older father purchased a SPIA as the sole owner and he was also the annuitant (the measuring life). He needed the income but also wanted his adult son to inherit the entire legacy portion if any remained at his death. The father named his son as the beneficiary. The father had a will where all the kids shared equally, although he wanted to carve out additional benefits for his son but didn't necessarily want his daughters to know about it. Believing the SPIA would pay the son directly upon his death, he made the

purchase. The initial payment was scheduled to start in nine months, when it was expected his income from a property lease would discontinue. The nine-month delay created a short deferral period that worked to increase the father's annual income vs. if he had just started the initial payment fifteen or so days following the SPIA purchase date (see "Variability" chapter).

In this case, a few months after the SPIA purchase date, the father slipped and fell at home. The father and contract owner who also happened to be the annuitant died about a month prior to the initial payment date. So what happened? The SPIA had a provision for an annuitant death prior to the first payment date. In this contract, the carrier voided the contract because a payment was never made and returned the entire purchase premium to the father's estate! The son eventually had to share the inheritance, meant solely for him, with his two sibling sisters. Not cool either.

The above two real-life cases are perfect examples highlight the very important role of a skilled annuity agent. Everyone has to know how the contracts work so a proper contract and variability (see "Variability" chapter) can be selected that meets the owner's expressed needs. More examples of interesting real life SPIA situations can be found in the "Anecdotes" chapter.

Other Provisions

Annuity or Settlement Options (found in deferred annuity contracts or life insurance policies): This is one of the income options in a deferred annuity contract or life insurance policy. The choices are limited but carry unique tax benefits (see the "Tax Implications" chapter). The carrier commits to minimum annuity rates for the available choices. The minimum annuity rates (monthly income) and their components are disclosed in your deferred annuity contract or life insurance policy. They are usually found in a chart at the back of the annuity contract or life insurance policy expressed as a dollar "rate per thousand of applied premium" (cash value) per month. This is very important, because in today's financial environment, often older, deferred annuity contract or life insurance policy annuity or settlement guaranteed rates exceed current rates available for a new SPIA. These provisions and their corresponding guarantees are also available to contract beneficiaries (see "Beneficiary Claims" in the "Tax Implications" chapter). When an annuity or settlement option is elected the carrier issues a "supplemental contract" to reflect new terms and conditions. Some carriers merely send a letter that acts as the contract. *However, it's better for consumers to receive an actual contract that outlines their property rights.*

A few SPIA contracts have other additional provisions not found in the traditional irrevocable SPIAs that we have, up until this time not discussed. These are offered by some carriers to theoretically make the contracts more attractive to consumers. However, federal income tax rules are not entirely clear regarding how such contracts might be treated. Most of these product marketing brochures have disclaimers, albeit in very small print and in obscure locations in the literature, disclosing there might be a consumer tax risk. This obscure and often obtuse disclosure is thought to cover the carrier's disclosure risk (lack thereof) if something blows up tax wise many years down the road after the contract purchase date. There will be more about tax issues in the "Tax Implications" chapter.

Payment Commutation: The most common additional provision is "payment commutation," aka contract withdrawal. This gives the consumer some ability to receive a lump-sum refund of some or even all of his or her purchase premium sometime after the SPIA purchase date. The provisions differ from contract to contract, and partial withdrawals effect the remaining payments in different ways depending on the contract. Some contracts permit several withdrawals over the life of the contract.

A payment advance of six months or less in one lump sum may also be an option under some SPIA contracts. This arrangement has the advantage of giving consumers a lump-sum cash amount without the possible adverse income tax consequences of a SPIA withdrawal. Depending on the provision, a consumer may make this election several times over the life of the contract. However, the size of the lump-sum payment advance is usually smaller compared to the potential size of a contract withdrawal from a payment commutation.

Nursing Home Confinement/Terminal Illness: A few SPIAs have nursing home confinement or terminal illness provisions that permit increased payment amounts for a short period of time or additional withdrawals or commutations.

There is a consumer cost for these provisions. The initial SPIA payment will be adjusted for the cost of these provisions compared to a SPIA from another carrier without these provisions.

The Application
The application is an integral part of the contract. In most cases, the application for the annuity is bound with the contract and is usually the last page. The application should be neat and well ordered. Today, for the most part, agents still prepare SPIA applications by hand, but with the advent of

electronic media, some carriers offer SPIA applications that can be prepared electronically. An electronic application helps agents to keep things neat and legible and prevents the omission of important information.

Applications should also not be submitted to the carrier with blank spaces just because the application section is not applicable to the particular case. For example, if there is a joint owner section on the application and the owner applies for single ownership, don't leave the joint owner section blank; instruct the agent to write "not applicable" or "NA" there. If you do not wish to nominate a "contingent beneficiary" on the application, then write "NA" in this section as well.

SPIA applications have "form numbers," which is super important. These numbers, in very small print, are usually found in the lower right-hand or left-hand corner of the application form. It discloses the proper form (application) to purchase your SPIA contract in your resident or purchase state. For example, the form number might read "1234-NY." This tells you, as a New York resident, the agent is using the proper form number. If you are a New York resident and you're purchasing the SPIA in a New York location, the form number should not be "4567-CA" or "8910-CT" or "IIPRC."

Sometimes the application will have an IIPRC designation. IIPRC stands for Interstate Insurance Product Regulation Commission. The IIPRC is a national organization, a multistate public entity established by the Interstate Insurance Compact ("compact"). The compact helps to bring certain standardizations to insurance products in general and in our case annuities in particular. The IIPRC allows companies to seek quicker product approvals from one source rather than making fifty separate state filings.

While not every state participates in the IIPRC, the IIPRC is now comprised of forty-three states. Carriers are not required to use the IIPRC, and some, depending on the annuity product, may elect not to use the IIPRC but instead choose to file for product approvals with the individual states. There are various reasons for this; for one reason, the product may be novel or have novel components the standardization feature of the IIPRC doesn't adequately allow for. Regardless, consumers are very well protected by the review and approval process of the IIPRC.

If the form number says "891011" or some other number and the state or IIPRC designation is not clear, make sure in the application owner signature area you record the date and the *actual physical location and state* where you signed the application; *never leave the physical location and state section blank.* If the form number for your state is wrong, the carrier will catch this and will not issue the contract. This is a safeguard against consumers accidently getting SPIA contracts not approved in the purchase state.

Another important area on the application is the "Remarks" section. This is a blank space on the application that should be used for several purposes. In this section, you could name an "irrevocable" beneficiary since most applications don't have check off boxes for this election. Again it's a powerful election, and most carriers don't want consumers or even agents making this choice too conveniently if they don't understand the full ramifications of the election.

After many years, people can become forgetful about the source of funds for their SPIA purchase, and the remarks section is a good place to record the source of funds, for example, from the ABC bank account number or the security brokerage IRA account number.

A very important notation can be made here for replacement transactions. The former carrier's name, annuity contract or life insurance carrier names and policy numbers, and "premium cost basis" (the purchase cost of the original annuity contract or life insurance policy less withdrawals and or losses) should go here as well. This dollar amount affects your tax benefit (see "Tax Implications" chapter). Over time, as replacements occur and for the owner to retain the ability to conduct proper tax planning, it is crucial to track the premium cost basis from annuity contract or life insurance policy to annuity contract. Many times this information is lost or the owner simply can't remember. The carriers have gotten better at tracking premium cost basis information for consumers, but it may not be accurate or not easily accessible to any agent or financial advisor reviewing the contract after it has been in force for many years (more about tax basis in the "Tax Implications" and "Brokerage" chapters).

Typically SPIA owners will need to also provide proof of date of birth for SPIAs with life-contingent payments, a resident address and not a PO Box, and driver's license or a state ID card for proof of identity. Other forms, although not part of the SPIA contract, might accompany the application, such as bank transfer request forms, replacement disclosures (if needed), and consumer disclosures of personal financial information. The agent's SPIA illustration the consumer may have to sign, depending on the practice of the carrier for the annuity purchase, usually accompanies the application (see "Brokerage" chapter).

Chapter Summary
• The immediate annuity contract outlines its particular parties and provisions, including the owner's rights, the free

look period, beneficiary privileges, what happens to the parties to the contract at times of death, payment amount and frequency, initial payment date and beneficiary elections, and a copy of the application.

• The state in which you purchase your annuity contract approves of its terms and conditions and regulates the insurance company that issues it to you. If there is a problem after you purchase your contract, the state will side with you regarding any valid complaint.

• The annuity application eventually becomes part of your contract and needs to be completed in its entirety with no blank spaces. It must be signed and dated by all the parties in the state where the applicant owner physically purchases the annuity. This prevents you from ending up with a contract not approved in the state of purchase.

PAYMENT VARIABILITY

"I speak Spanish to God, Italian to women, French to men, and German when I talk to my horse."
—*Charles V*

Introduction

Payment variability is what makes the SPIA world go round. While the contract itself cannot be changed (see the "Contract" chapter), the contract has to offer payment flexibility and variable components in order to accommodate the particular needs and wants of the consumer purchasing the contract. However, once the consumer selects the payment variability, it is inscribed on the deceleration page of the contract. Unless the payment variability is changed during the free look period, it will become, like the contract, equally intractable. This is why the free look review period is important (see the "Contract" chapter).

However, SPIA carrier payment variability selection offerings vary widely from carrier to carrier. Some carriers only offer "standard" selections or very limited selections, and then there are a few carriers that offer a wide range of selections. Just like in other forms of insurance, some carriers are more specialized in the SPIAs than others. A good SPIA agent will know the SPIA "marketplace" and also rely on third party SPIA brokers such as brokerage general agents (BGAs) or insurance marketing organizations (IMOs) to locate the proper contract and payment variability for their case.

Besides making SPIA payment price comparisons, agents scour the SPIA market every day searching for SPIA payment variability, trying to come up with a SPIA solution for a particular case, and perhaps, not finding a single contract to do the job, they may have to utilize several contracts from different carriers to accomplish their goal (see the "Brokerage" chapter). Typically, for retail commercial SPIAs, there is only one payment structure per contract, which is another reason why the agent might have to use multiple SPIA contracts.

Payment variability pricing is driven primarily by interest rates, and in some cases, depending on the type of payment, the age and gender of the annuitant. The other factors that drive payment variability pricing among others are agent commissions, company operating expenses, investments, profitability, and SPIA contract optional features. There is little to no pricing transparency about how any one carrier prices its SPIA payment variability, which is another reason why consumers should rely on their agents for price and contract comparisons. *It is not sufficient to only examine a pricing comparison chart. You really have to know the contract (see the "Contract" chapter) because contracts have varying features, terms and conditions.*

There are basically two types of SPIA payments, which are period certain and life-contingent. Notice I did not say lifetime. Lifetime implies the SPIA payment continues over the life of an individual(s) regardless of his or her eventual attained age. While some SPIA payments do just that, there are other life-contingent payments that only pay on but not after certain dates, even if you are still alive. There will be more about these kinds of life-contingent payments later.

Variability Selections (Payment Structures)
These are the most common SPIA structures.

Period-Certain Only aka Term-Certain Only is a payment duration ranging five to thirty years made to owners and their beneficiaries. The beneficiary(s) inherits unpaid payments when the annuitant dies.

Lifetime Only aka "Straight Life" is a payment duration for your entire lifetime (single life) or joint lifetimes (joint life) regardless of how long you or both of you live, depending on the case. The contract terminates when you die, or in the case of joint lifetimes, when the last annuitant dies, and there is no payment beneficiary(s). In the case of joint lifetimes, this is called 100 percent survivorship life.

Temporary Life is a payment duration ranging five to twenty years with a single life contingency. You have to be alive on each payment date to receive that payment. If you survive the duration, the payment will stop. If you die during the payment duration, the contract terminates and there are no payment beneficiary(s).

Period Certain and Life is a payment with some of each of the above elements: a period-certain duration for five to fifty years and then also a single or joint lifetime payment provision. In the case of joint lifetimes, this is called 100 percent survivorship life.

Period Certain and Life Cash or Installment Refund is single or joint lifetime payment designed to pay at least the amount equal to the purchase premium to either the single or joint lifetime annuitants or the beneficiary(s) if the single annuitant or both annuitants, depending on the case, don't survive long enough to collect the entire purchase premium. For a cash refund, it's a single lump-sum balance payment. For installment refund, it is a continuation of the payment until at least the entire purchase premium has been paid.

Pension Joint aka Survivorship Life Reduction is a payment with or without a certain period, after the period-certain period (if any) concludes, the payment reduces by some preset percentage when the first in line primary annuitant life dies. The survivorship amount might be 75 percent, 50 percent, or some other amount of the payment. This payment structure is typically used for IRAs and qualified retirement plans, but it can also be used in other nonretirement plan cases.

Survivorship Life Reduction is a payment, with or without a certain period, after the period-certain period (if any) concludes the payment reduces by some preset percentage when either; the first in line primary annuitant *or* second in line secondary annuitant life dies. The survivorship amount might be 75 percent or 50 percent or some other amount of the payment.

True Joint while not a common offered payment, it produces the highest annual income of any lifetime SPIA structure. This is a joint, lifetime-only "straight life" payment and pays for as long as both annuitants live. However, because there is no survivorship, the contract terminates at the first death of any joint annuitant, and there is no contract beneficiary(s).

Cost of Living Adjustment (COLA) is a payment provision that may be attached to any of the above SPIA payments, depending on the offerings of the particular carrier. COLAs are usually annual, consecutive payment adjustments over the life of the contract. COLAs are expressed as a compounded or simple interest percentage rate of the payment. COLAs permit consumers to create an internal payment deferral because future payments are greater than the initial payment. A few carriers still offer "payment step-ups." This is a payment increase occurring at three, five, ten and so on year increments, depending on the contract.

Payment Modes; there are four; monthly, quarterly, semiannual, or annual. The payment mode is usually paid at the modal period as measured from the purchase date. For example, the monthly payment is paid after thirty days, the quarterly payment is paid after ninety days, and so on. The initial modal payment can also be made on the contract issue date. In this instance, there is no deferral period between the annuity purchase date and the initial annuity payment. However, depending on the carrier and SPIA you could make the monthly payment after six months or even up to one year from the purchase date. This is called an "off modal" payment and may create an internal payment deferral if the modal payment is made at a much later date than normal. In this case, the deferred payment will be greater than if the payment were made at its normal time. For example, if the monthly modal payment is made after a one-year deferral as opposed to being made after thirty days, the one-year deferral will cause the monthly payment to be greater (see the "Brokerage" chapter for why this might be done). The discussion of off-modal payments has a huge impact today when we discuss deferred income annuity (DIA) contracts in which initial payments can be deferred for up to thirty years (see the "When Worlds Collide" chapter).

Variability Pricing
Now that variability has been introduced, this is a good point to start the discussion of SPIA pricing associated with that variability relative to any particular consumer who purchases a contract. This is the premium purchase cost.

Interest Rates

SPIA contracts exclusively containing period-certain-only payments are priced primarily as a function of the interest rate environment at the time of contract issue. Sometimes these contracts are referred to as "interest only" SPIAs. While annuitant age and gender impact the pricing of other SPIAs, they have no impact on contracts comprised solely of period-certain-only payments.

All SPIAs utilize more than one interest rate to price their payments. This makes sense because payments can be made over several decades. Interest rates available in the corporate or government bond debt market, at any given time at the SPIA purchase date, are normally lower at shorter durations of five to ten years vs. longer durations of thirty to forty years. For example, in a "normal" interest rate environment, the average five, ten, fifteen, thirty, and forty-year interest rates might be 1.30 percent, 2.50 percent, 3.05 percent, 3.60 percent and 3.25 percent, respectively. Interest rates increase as the years in the future become further away from the present. Then, at some much later time, usually after thirty years or so, interest rates begin to taper off.

If you were to graph these rates in addition to all the other in-between years' rates (see Interest Rates vs Years) for a forty-year period-certain only SPIA, you would form a bell-shaped curve. The curve, starting in the early years with lower interest rates, would slowly rise from left to right as the SPIA payment duration lengthened to reflect the higher interest rates in the later years. Because all interest rates, regardless of duration, constantly shift, from day to day, SPIA period-certain only premium purchase prices (cost) or payments can change daily.

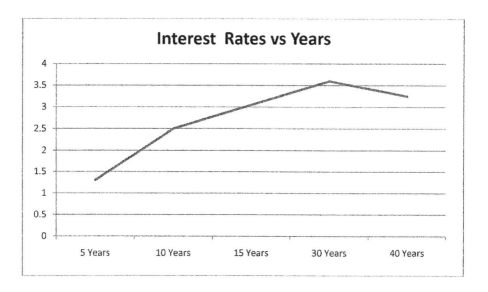

However, because today's business climate is producing ultra-low interest rates, payments from period-certain-only contracts are also low relative to where they would be if the interest rate market was more generous and offered high interest rates like in prior years.

For example, given a $50,000 purchase cost, the current monthly payments (at writing date) for a 120 payment (ten-year) and a 60 payment (five-year) period-certain only annuity are $445 and $835, respectively. The five-year annuity has a higher monthly payment compared to the ten-year annuity because it's paid over a shorter duration.

In a more normal interest rate environment from the early to late 1990s, assuming a 5.50 percent average interest rate, these same annuities might produce $537 and $948, respectively. Over their respective time periods, this amounts to a lot of lost interest. The differences of $92 ($537 − $445) and $113 ($948 − $835) per month is $11,040 ($92 x 120) and $6,780 ($113 x 60), respectively, over the life of the contracts. In this manner, you can see the impact of the current ultra-low interest rate environment on the annuity market in the loss of interest income.

Note: In insurance company lingo, these monthly payment rates might be quoted as functions of per thousand of premium cost. For example, the 120-month (ten-year) period-certain annuity might be quoted at a rate of $8.90 per thousand of premium cost. This is calculated by the monthly payment $445 / 50 ($50,000).

Mortality

Because you can't put mortality into a hand-held business or financial calculator, this is the toughest SPIA pricing concept consumers and agents struggle with. Since SPIAs with life-contingent payments terminate when annuitants die, it's difficult to wrap your head around how that impacts payment pricing and that this effect can even be calculated. While carriers don't know which annuitants will die, they know some will die. The pricing concept based upon annuitant death potential stretches back through the history of annuity time (see "History" chapter), and it determines annuity payment pricing or the annuity purchase cost, depending on the case. Another book could be written on mortality. But it is safe to say the carrier makes an estimate about how many annuitants might die in any given year. This estimate helps to determine the cost and annuity payment of any given annuity with a life contingency.

Since carriers know they only have to worry about annuity payments to survivors, these carriers can ignore annuitants they believe will not survive. Because payments with life contingencies only impact survivors, carriers can pay greater payments or reduce premium costs for any given payment since they will have extra money derived from annuitants that die early.

Let's look at how interest and mortality work together to determine an annuity payment at the end of one year for six, single male annuitants, aged eighty-five. They each pay a $1,000 premium, and the insurance company can credit them 3.00 percent interest. The insurance company is going to earn 5.00 percent on this premium. So, the carrier is anxious to issue this contract. The carrier also assumes one of these six annuitants will not survive to the end of the year. So, the carrier only has to worry about paying five survivors.

At the end of the year, the carrier is on the hook to return the original $1,000 premium cost plus $30 (3 percent interest) or $1,030 to each annuitant. However, when the carrier initially issues the annuity contract, they assume one of the annuitants is going to die so they will not have to make one of the $1,030 payments. What becomes of this $1,030? It's shared with the surviving five annuitants. If one is really going to die prior to end of the year, why wait to share it at the end of the year? The carrier just promises it up front to all six annuitants who purchase such a contract. If they are going to have an extra $1,030 and there are going to be five survivors, then each annuitant gets an extra $206 ($1,030 / 5)! Therefore, the total promised payment to all six initial annuitants is the original $1,030 plus the mortality credit/sharing payment of $206 for a total of $1,236.

It's that simple, and the basis for how a mortality contingency is factored into the determination of the annuity payment, or conversely, it's factored into the annuity premium purchase cost. The following Annuity Payment Calculation Table 1 illustrates the relationship interaction of interest rates and mortality assumptions.

Annuity Payment Calculation Table 1

Male Purchase Date Age	Annuity Purchase Cost Today For Each Male	3% Annual Interest Credited Guaranteed by The Carrier ($1,000 x 3%)	Mortality Credit/Sharing Guaranteed by the Carrier Assuming One Death ($1,030/5 - Survivors)	Total Annuity Payment Guaranteed by the Carrier at the Annuity Purchase Date to Each Annuitant After One year ($1,000 + $30+ $206)
85	$1,000	$30	$206	$1,236

In the above case, each annuitant, in exchange for their $1,000 premium cost, is promised a payment of $1,236 at the end of the year. This is a 23.60 percent increase ($236 / $1,000) over the payment cost.

How much interest did these annuitants earn on their money? The answer is 3.00 percent. The earnings difference is chalked up to the mortality credit sharing, merely because they survived to the end of the year. This is one reason why these annuities with life contingencies have become so popular in today's repressive interest rate environment. Surviving individuals who now can't earn favorable returns due to low interest rates or who can't tolerate stock market risk need the relatively high-guaranteed payments that such contracts produce.

But what happens if the carriers' estimates are wrong and none of the above initial six annuitants die? Since all initial six annuitants were promised $1,236 the carrier has to come up with the additional $1,236 out of their own pocket, ouch! This is why insurance carriers are subject to State regulations and are required to post financial reserves so that money is there to make up for any miscalculations in order to make their guaranteed payments (more about this in the "Protection" chapter).

OK, but what if two of the annuitants in our example die? In this case, the carrier only has to make three $1,236 payments. Did the carrier get a "windfall"? No, not really because the typical annuity, unlike in this example, is paid over long durations, possibly decades. Due to carrier estimate errors, gains in any one year are needed to offset possible losses in the future years when the carriers' experience might be different.

Age and Gender

Two important elements help determine life-contingent annuity payment variability pricing are age and gender. The carrier calculates the older you are, the closer you are to death. This makes sense from a strictly aging standpoint. As the rate of death increases, there will be more payment forfeitures from dying annuitants, and the higher the initial payment guarantees can be made to all annuitants.

Studies show women, in general, live longer than men. Therefore, when the same life-contingent annuity contracts are considered, given equal premium costs, and since men generally die earlier than women of the same age, men receive larger annuity payments or conversely better annuity purchase costs.

Annuity Impaired Risk

Another reason to consider purchasing SPIAs and singularly unique to SPIAs with life-contingent annuity payments is annuitant-impaired risk underwriting. This is a pricing technique whereby the carrier takes into consideration the ill health and or injuries of the annuitant. While this part of the SPIA market, and carrier availability, was more robust when interest rates were higher, currently there are only a couple of carriers who will consider annuitant ill health or injuries on the SPIA payment pricing decision.

An individual who has been medically rated and moves up to a higher mortality class receives better annuity pricing than they would normally receive for their chronological age and gender. An annuitant age sixty-five who moves into the age eighty-five class (rated age) after they have been evaluated by the carrier, simply receives higher life-contingent SPIA payments for any given premium or conversely lower SPIA costs for any given payment.

This is important because individuals who are disabled because of their health or injuries are some of the most fragile elements of our society. They can't afford financial loss because they have reduced ability to generate wage income and typically can't comfortably absorb financial risks associated with the stock market or losses associated with other financial products like mutual funds and savings accounts or funds dissipation risks. Their needs for guaranteed and also generous income sources are paramount (see "Protection" chapter).

SPIAs to the rescue! To illustrate increased mortality assumptions and the impact on SPIA pricing, let's modify our assumptions of the SPIA purchase and now assume two instead of one of the six males aged eighty-five will die. This actually increases SPIA payments (see the Table 2 below).

Annuity Payment Calculation Table 2 (Impaired Risk)

Male Purchase Date Age	Annuity Purchase Cost Today For Each Male	3% Annual Interest Credited Guaranteed by The Carrier ($1,000 x 3%)	Mortality Credit/Sharing Guaranteed by the Carrier Assuming Two Deaths ($2,060/4 - Survivors)	Total Annuity Payment Guaranteed by the Carrier at the Annuity Purchase Date to Each Annuitant After One year ($1,000 + $30+ $515)
85	$1,000	$30	$515	$1,545

In this case, there are two assumed deaths and an extra $2,060 ($1,030 x 2). Since there are four survivors, each gets an extra $515 ($2,060/4). In this case, the insurance company can initially promise all six annuitants a $1,545 payment at the end of the year compared to the $1,236 for one annuitant death assumption because they think two annuitants rated age eighty-five aren't going to make it to the end of the year.

If an annuitant-impaired risk pricing evaluation is to be considered, the agent must notify the carrier and send documents stating the annuitant's health and injury history, current medical condition, and prognosis. These documents could be test results, prescription drug usage, and hospital discharge summaries. An insurance company underwriter will evaluate the annuitant's medical history and make a decision about how this medical history and prognosis will affect the carriers SPIA payment pricing. An underwriter is a carrier employee who evaluates these kinds of risks. Typically, this decision will hold for about six months, which is enough time to accommodate a SPIA purchase. If a SPIA purchase doesn't take place within this time, typically, a new set of medical records have to be submitted.

This SPIA pricing technique is primarily used in the structured settlement annuity industry because annuity contracts are often purchased to settle lawsuits and pay damage awards in order to provide income for sick or disabled individuals who suffered some injury.

The agent has to make a judgment call about the benefit of such a SPIA. While the annuitant benefits from better life-contingent annuity pricing, if the annuitant health is too impaired he or she may only survive a few years. If this might be the case then other factors will need to be weighed in the SPIA purchase decision (see "Protection" chapter). For example, instead of purchasing a full lifetime SPIA, perhaps the more suitable purchase might be a short duration temporary life contract for just five years. The amount of premium for any given monthly payment is significantly reduced compared to purchasing a full lifetime only annuity, and the annuitant still receives the benefit of impaired risk underwriting on his or her annuity purchase (see "Brokerage" chapter).

If the annuitant might only survive a few of years, then the protection benefit (anti-dissipation) will have to be highly weighted in the SPIA purchase decision for such a transaction to make financial sense (see "Protection" chapter).

State Premium Tax and Other Carrier Expenses

Other things that affect carrier SPIA payment variability pricing are state-imposed premium taxes and carrier expenses.

A premium purchase tax is imposed by a few states on their resident citizens who purchase SPIA contracts. At this time, the annuity premium tax states are California, Maine, Nevada, South Dakota, Virgin Islands, West Virginia, and Wyoming. The premium tax rate differs from state to state. For example, the premium tax in California is 2.35 percent of the SPIA premium purchase cost. If the SPIA premium purchase cost is $50,000, then the tax is $1,175 ($50,000 x 2.35 percent). After the imposition of this tax, the annuitant only has the balance or $48,825 to apply to the annuity purchase cost because the carrier sent $1,175 to the state. This is one reason why an annuitant with residences in both California and Florida might decide to purchase his or her SPIA contract in Florida.

Carrier expenses are harder to estimate because there are so many different kinds, including agent commissions, and how each one contributes to annuity purchase cost determination as a whole. Sometimes it can be expressed as a "load" on the premium cost. For example, after all other cost elements are determined and a premium cost is reached, the carrier might just add another flat 3 percent to the premium cost. This is dependent on how the carrier handles factoring in their costs.

Another way of expressing company expenses is in the interest rates used to credit SPIA interest. For example, the carrier uses a 3.00 percent rate to credit interest in our example because the carrier can only earn 5.00 percent and the 2.00 percent (5 percent – 3 percent) difference, the margin, is needed to cover the carriers' expenses and earn an expected profit. If the carriers' expenses were lower, for example, the carrier may only need to earn 1.50 percent to cover expenses and earn the same expected profit. In that case, the carrier SPIA purchase cost pricing might grant annuitants a 3.50 percent interest rate and effectively increase the annuitant's SPIA payment because there will be more interest earnings.

Frustrating consumer SPIA purchase decisions and some SPIA agents, carrier expenses, interest rates and their assumptions regarding how many annuitants will die in any given year is not disclosed to the consumer. Carriers believe this is all proprietary information that needs to be withheld from nosey carrier competitors.

Given all the above, plus differences from contract to contract in the terms and conditions, it is really impossible to know why one SPIA carrier pays a larger payment or offers a lower purchase cost compared to another carrier. This is why many agents look at SPIA cost comparisons so nearly like contracts can be evaluated for purchase considerations. This is another excellent reason to use a skilled SPIA agent. The key is SPIA contracts need to be nearly similar for this evaluation to have any meaning. Typically only experienced SPIA agents have sufficient skills to make comparisons between competing contracts.

Federal Intervention
While federal intervention in SPIA matters is primarily driven by income tax concerns, it affects SPIA variability and will be discussed at length in the "Tax Implications" chapter. There is significant tax benefits associated with SPIA contracts. For those SPIA contracts that are also individual retirement arrangements (IRAs) or pension fund or retirement plan contracts, the federal government limits consumer SPIA payment variability selections. For now, in this chapter, it's just sufficient to mention.

Chapter Summary
• SPIA payment options include period certain only, single or joint life only, period certain and single or joint life with and without payment reductions, temporary life, true joint, and cost of living adjustments (COLAs) paid over durations of five to fifty years. Payment frequencies can be monthly, quarterly, semiannual, or annual and can be paid any time within the initial twelve months or further deferred out to thirty years. Very few carriers provide all this variability; it may be necessary to work with several to obtain the desired payment variability combination.

• Payment variability pricing is determined by interest rates, mortality assumptions, company expenses and profit expectations, and state premium taxes. Depending on the circumstance, an annuitant-impaired risk may provide greater payments for any given premium or provide a lower purchase cost for any given payment.

TAX IMPLICATIONS

"To tax and to please, no more than to
love and be wise, is not given to men."
– *Edmund Burke, Political Philosopher*

Introduction
Throughout this book, it's my contention tax benefits of SPIA
ownership are only second to safety as the primary reason
to purchase a SPIA (see "Protection" chapter). As you will
see, there are significant tax benefits for the owner(s) and
also their beneficiary(s) who might become the new contract
owners. While I will steer as clear as possible away from tax
benefits of deferred annuity contracts and life insurance policies, they are inevitably linked to SPIA contracts. The SPIA
contract, besides being a cash purchase, can also be the
income component of an existing deferred annuity contract or
life insurance policy. To some degree, this chapter is joined at
the hip to the "Brokerage" chapter.

Owner's Federal Income Tax
Over the years, the IRS has struggled developing income
tax policy for SPIA contracts. SPIA tax policy has morphed
over several decades and since the imposition of income
tax itself. SPIAs aren't designed like other financial products; they don't have cash balances. There is no convenient
or easily measurable current value. So, as we will see, they
have their own unique income tax rules.

Generally, because there are so many interdependent elements, it isn't wise to dispense personal income tax advice. Everyone is slightly different, and what affects one person a certain way income tax wise way may not have the same effect on another. Certainly, you should always discuss your big income tax picture with an income tax professional. However, that doesn't mean a SPIA agent should shy away from income specific "tax facts" directly associated with SPIAs. First of all, for federal income tax purposes, "taxable" SPIA income is classified as "ordinary income." Ordinary income includes all forms of any income other than income that can be defined as "capital gains" income, which is investment income.

Federal Penalty
Normally, the IRS penalizes all annuity taxable income at a rate of 10 percent if the contract owner receives it prior to age fifty-nine and a half. However, for SPIAs, as long as the initial payment date falls within one year of the SPIA purchase date, SPIA contracts are exempt from the penalty.

Then again, if the SPIA is funded via a 1035 exchange from a deferred annuity that is more than one year old, the one-year exception attaches to the original deferred annuity, and this SPIA income is subject to the penalty. But if the SPIA income is paid over the annuitant's lifetime, then it is not subject to the penalty in any way.

Nonqualified vs. Qualified Contracts
SPIA contracts can be purchased with two types of money: SPIAs purchased with money on which you have already paid income taxes on is post tax money. Typically this money resides in a personal checking, savings, or stockbrokerage account. These contracts are called "nonqualified"

money contracts. SPIAs purchased with money from individual retirement arrangements (IRAs) or other pension or retirement plan sources that have not yet been taxed are pretax monies. These contracts are called "qualified" money contracts. Because there are two types of money purchase contracts, nonqualified and qualified, there are two sets of federal income tax rules.

State Premium Tax

A few states assess a premium tax on their state residents against the SPIA purchase premium. This tax reduces the ultimate purchase amount, and the insurance company collects the tax and then forwards it to the state. States charge different tax rates, depending if the SPIA premium is nonqualified or qualified funds. Typically, when the agent presents the SPIA illustration to you during the purchase process (see "Brokerage" chapter), the agent's SPIA illustration will usually indicate if a premium tax is included and what the tax rate is. States with annuity premium taxes include California, Maine, Nevada, South Dakota, West Virginia, and Wyoming.

Nonqualified Purchase Premium

The single most important income tax element of a non-qualified SPIA contract to track is its "cost basis" also known as "tax basis." The cost basis is important because you only have to pay income tax on SPIA income that exceeds your premium cost. The cost basis is simply the amount of money you paid for the contract.

In fact, a good SPIA agent will record the cost basis in the remarks section of the application. This is very important because as the years progress, people forget what they paid for their contract. If the amount is recorded on the application, they or some future agent or financial advisor can easily ascertain the cost basis. Cost basis usage planning is what makes these contracts "sing" and what helps separate a good SPIA agent from a great one. The cost basis tracking isn't too difficult if you are purchasing the contract with cash. For example, if I purchase a SPIA contract for $50,000 with funds from my non-IRA checking account then my cost basis is $50,000.

1035 Exchange
An annuity contract or life insurance policy 1035 exchange is a federal income tax provision where any gains from the prior annuity contract or life insurance policy, along with its corresponding cost basis, are transferred to a new annuity contract without current income taxation. This exchange is sometimes called a "replacement" because a former annuity contract or life insurance policy is replaced with a new annuity contract. This transaction can be for a complete or partial replacement.

Let's say several years ago I purchased a deferred annuity contract for $35,000, and then when the contract had cash surrender value of $50,000, I transferred it to a new SPIA contract. While my purchase cost is $50,000 for the SPIA contract, my cost basis is only $35,000, and at the transfer and replacement date, my $15,000 gain continues its income tax deferral. Or, for example, I paid $60,000 for the deferred annuity contract and because it lost money due to the stock market (a variable deferred annuity), I only transferred $50,000, but my cost basis is still $60,000!

If instead, I had an old life insurance policy I purchased in my forties, and now in my sixties the policy has a cash or surrender value of $10,000, it might be I paid a total of

$40,000 in life premiums over the decades, and the cost basis is $40,000.

We will see in the "Brokerage" chapter how one can really take advantage of the tax breaks associated with cost basis and SPIA contracts.

The above examples are for entire exchanges and replacements, but what about partial exchanges and replacements by 1035 exchange. For years the IRS fought against the concept of "partial" 1035 exchange, thinking it could lead to tax abusive situations, and it's only in the last several years the IRS relented with rules that control the taxability of the distributions that follow partial 1035 exchange (these distributions will be discussed later).

However, for partial deferred annuity exchange regarding the premium purchase cost, the IRS implemented a pro rata rule that basically says the cost basis allocated to the new SPIA contract is in direct proportion to the funds transferred. This is sometimes referred to as the cream-in-coffee rule.

Like cream in coffee, once you have nontaxable cost basis combined with untaxed interest accumulations, they cannot be separated due to a 1035 exchange or even a SPIA commutation (see "Third Parties" chapter). Taking my first example, if I instead transfer via a 1035 exchange $25,000, or half of my $50,000 contract, with a cost basis of $35,000, then half ($17,500) of my cost basis transfers to the new SPIA contract as well. My remaining deferred annuity contract now has a cash surrender value of $25,000 and a cost basis of $17,500 while my new SPIA contract has a premium purchase cost of $25,000 with a cost basis of $17,500.

The sending insurance company remits a report to the receiving insurance company about the cost basis amount.

However, for very old, deferred annuity contracts that have been transferred from carrier to carrier over the decades, this important cost-basis information may have been mis-reported, or worse, just lost. For example, in order to issue the new annuity deferred contract with as few hang-ups as possible, if the cost basis report information doesn't arrive from the sending carrier, the current carrier often just reports a $0 cost basis in order to quickly issue the new contract. This shifts the entire correct income tax reporting burden to the consumer. Because income from a deferred annuity contract is typically not taken until later in life, the mistake often does not rear its ugly head until it is too late to determine the correct tax basis.

Because a SPIA can usually be purchased as a component of a deferred annuity contract or life insurance policy (see "Contract" chapter), the same tax rules regarding cost basis also apply. For example, I may own a current deferred annuity contract or life insurance policy and elect to exercise the annuity option available to me in my existing annuity contract or life insurance policy.

These features are found in your deferred annuity contract or life insurance policy and are usually called "annuity options" or "settlement options." The choices are limited but carry the weight of certain insurance company rate guarantees. If you have an older contract or policy issued when interest rates were much higher than the current rates, and you wish to make one of the annuity or settlement option elections, it would behoove you to check with the current carrier and the rates in your deferred annuity contract or life insurance policy before purchasing a new SPIA from a different company.

As you can begin to see, since SPIA income is only taxed to the extent income exceeds the contract's cost basis, if optimal annuity planning is done, there is ample room to reap substantial income tax benefits (see "Brokerage" chapter).

Nonqualified Income

The IRS has a formula for the taxation of SPIA income. Recalling our basic income tax rule, SPIA income is only taxed to the extent it exceeds the SPIA cost basis. This tax benefit lies in how the IRS calculates the cost basis amount recognized and paid in any given year. The rule is: the SPIA cost basis is gradually allocated over the payment duration of the annuity contract. This duration can be expressed over the payment duration of the contract or even over the annuitant's life expectancy, as defined by the IRS.

For example, if I purchase my $60,000 SPIA contract and the cost basis is also $60,000 and the payment duration is ten years or 120 months (period-certain; see "Variability" chapter), starting thirty days from the purchase date, my nontaxable monthly income is $500 ($60,000/120). If the monthly income is $535, then $35 is the taxable portion produced by the SPIA. Over the course of one tax year, this contract produces $420 ($35 x 12) of annual taxable income; the other $6,000 ($500 x 12) of income is not taxable.

Many times on SPIA agent computer-generated illustrations used during the sale and presentation process, this nontaxable share is expressed as a percentage of the total income (see "Brokerage" chapter). In this case, since the monthly nontaxable portion is $500 and the total monthly income is $535, the nontaxable or income "excludable" portion is 93.46 percent ($500 / $535).

In another case, using the above purchase facts, if I'm age sixty-five and I purchase a "lifetime" life-only (see

"Variability" chapter) SPIA, then the IRS life expectancy table (Table V) says I get to use twenty years (240 months) as the expected annuity payment duration. In this IRS table, it doesn't matter if I am a male or female. Therefore, using the above example, my nontaxable monthly income is $250 ($60,000 / 240). At current SPIA rates, a male produces about $315 per month and a female produces about $295 per month.

Therefore, for a male, the taxable SPIA income is $65 ($315 – $250) per month and for a female it's $45 ($295 – $250) per month. In these cases, the income excluded, nontaxable portion is 79.37 percent ($250 / $315) and 84.75 percent ($250 / $295) for the male and female respectively.

In this case, the male receives a little more taxable income than the female because males, in general, don't live as long females and therefore their mortality credits are larger than female credits at any given age (see "Payment Variability" chapter). However, the nontaxable portion of $250 remains the same for each.

Nonqualified Income (Partial Exchanges/ Replacements)

When SPIA contracts are funded with proceeds of a 1035 partial exchange or replacement transaction from deferred annuity contract, the tax rules are slightly different. In these cases in order for the transaction to qualify under the IRS rules for 1035 exchanges, the initial SPIA payment date must occur at least six months or later, following the trans-action purchase date. This IRS rule was enacted to prevent abusive tax transactions.

Normally "withdrawals" from deferred annuity contracts are taxed as withdrawals of interest to the extent of the deferred annuity contract gains. Because interest earnings have to follow the annuity purchase cost, as a natural course, these withdrawals are called "last in first out" (LIFO)*. If I have a deferred annuity contract with a cost basis of $35,000 and a cash value of $50,000 and I start a $200 monthly withdrawal, this amount is entirely taxable because I have $15,000 ($50,000 – $35,000) of untaxed gains, and the contract is also earning some current income. The $200 taxable monthly withdrawal is deemed for income tax purposes to come from my untaxed deferred gains. When my entire $15,000 gain is depleted, along with any current gains, then my withdrawals will not be subject to income tax.

The obvious tax benefit is I could just do a partial 1035 exchange for the same $200 monthly income and reap the SPIA tax benefit (see "Brokerage" chapter). To make these transactions less attractive, the IRS instituted a minimal six month income delay period.

Instead of making that $200 monthly "withdrawal," I could purchase a SPIA, using a partial 1035 exchange from a deferred annuity for a six-year (seventy-two month) period-certain SPIA that produces a $200 monthly benefit. In this case, such a SPIA would cost $14,100, considering the initial payment starts six months following the purchase date.

If my original deferred annuity cost basis is $35,000, the SPIAs cost basis is $9,870 [($14,100 / $50,000) x $35,000] under the pro rata rule. But because of the SPIA tax rule, the premium cost basis, $9,870, divided by the seventy-two month payment duration means $137.08 of the $200 SPIA payment is not taxable! In this case, the SPIA permits me the same level of income while simultaneously improving my tax savings. However, the interest rate I earn on the SPIA over this six-year duration will invariably be different than the interest rate earned on the deferred annuity contract's cash balance over the same period.

Nonqualified Income (Partial Annuitization)

Annuitization is an industry term also often used to describe an immediate annuity. I introduce the word here because the income tax rules for partial annuitization are slightly different than for the income tax treatment for SPIAs purchased by partial 1035 exchanges.

In these cases, the existing deferred annuity contract is partially annuitized. The deferred annuity carrier just takes a portion of the existing deferred annuity contract cash value and uses it to fund an annuity or settlement option (immediate annuity) described in the deferred annuity contract (see "Contract" chapter). The cost basis is distributed via the pro rata technique.

The carrier issues what is usually called a "supplemental" contract. The supplemental contract describes the annuity income option or settlement option terms and conditions. At this point the supplemental contract controls the property rights. This is important for later and explained in the "Brokerage" chapter. Because of state-imposed rules, when partial annuitization occurs, the carrier has to pay the better of the guaranteed annuity rates as stipulated by his or her deferred contract or the current SPIA rate for the desired SPIA.

In addition, if the annuity duration is ten years or longer or over the life or joint life of the annuitant(s), the initial payment date does not have to be deferred six months, but it can start at any time within the first contract year.

Beneficiaries Who Become Owners

One of the interesting income tax provisions is; when the annuitant dies, not only do the remaining annuity payments (if any) go to the contract beneficiary; he or she also receives the remaining cost basis. Some SPIA contracts permit the beneficiary(s) to commute the remaining payments in lieu of receiving them as scheduled. If the scheduled payments continue, the beneficiary becomes the new contract owner.

For SPIAs that are period-certain-only in which the beneficiary inherits the scheduled payments, the beneficiary declares income in the same manner as the former owner. In other words, if out of the above $200 monthly payment $137.08 is not taxable, the beneficiary gets the same treatment and only receives a 1099 for the difference of $62.92, just the same as the former owner.

However, let's just change the SPIA, and the beneficiary tax treatment becomes entirely different. Let's say the owner purchased a SPIA for twenty years period-certain, and then for lifetime thereafter. This SPIA is called period-certain and life (see "Variability" chapter). If the father owner dies after five years, his beneficiary stands to inherit the remaining fifteen schedule years under the contract. Wonder upon wonder, in this case the beneficiary gets a tax break because he or she gets to use the entire remaining SPIA cost basis first!

This has important wealth transitioning strategies we will see more of in the "Brokerage" chapter.

Let's look at an example: Father, age eighty, purchases a twenty-year period-certain and lifetime thereafter SPIA and names his adult child, age fifty-five, as the beneficiary of the contract. The father dies at age eighty-five and his child inherits the remaining fifteen contract years or 180 monthly payments. The father's purchase cost was $50,000 and the monthly payment is $ 260.00 with $ 206.00 being the nontaxable portion. After five years, at the father's death, he received $12,360 ($206 x 60) of the annuity purchase cost. Therefore the cost basis balance, $37,640 ($50,000 - $12,360), remained to be paid at his death.

Since the child inherits the $260 monthly payment, none of this payment is taxable for about 144 months, or twelve years ($37,640 / $260). Then in the next three years, after all the premium purchase cost has been paid, the SPIA payment becomes 100 percent taxable to the child to finish out the remaining fifteen years due to him after the father died.

This has important income tax implications for the adult child. If the adult child is working, now at age sixty when the father dies, in their prime earning years and high tax bracket years, it gives the child nontaxable income until such a time, as they themselves are retired and in a much lower income tax bracket. In this example, the child will not start paying income taxes until they are age seventy-two (age sixty when father died + twelve nontaxable years). Then from age seventy-three to seventy-five (the next three years), the child's annuity income is 100 percent taxable.

For SPIAs that have joint annuitants, the survivor annuitant, who becomes the new owner, receives the same taxable income as the former owner. For a joint annuitant SPIA with period-certain payments, the beneficiary of such contracts also receive the same nontaxable treatment, but in this case both annuitants would have to die with remaining unpaid period-certain payments.

Let's look at another example where the child inherits but can't recover all the premium cost. Father, age eighty, purchases a $50,000 seven-year period-certain and lifetime thereafter SPIA with a monthly payment of $395, and $385 is not taxable. The father dies after two years after receiving $9,240 ($385 x 24 months) of the annuity purchase cost.

The remaining purchase cost is $40,760 ($50,000 – $9,240). The adult child stands to inherit sixty monthly scheduled payments of $395 each. The total payments are

$23,700 ($395 x 60), and all are not taxable because the total payments of $23,700 are less than the total remaining purchase cost of $40,760 (cost basis).

So, what becomes of the $17,060 difference ($40,760 cost basis less the total remaining payments of $23,700)? This becomes a tax loss on the son's income tax return as a tax deduction for "lost insurance premiums," and this deduction is usually taken in the miscellaneous itemized deduction area on page 2 of the 1040 Federal tax return. However there is a 2 percent of adjusted gross income (AIG) floor limitation.

If the father instead purchased a lifetime only "straight life" (see "Variability" chapter) SPIA for $50,000 and died after only receiving $5,000 premium cost because there are no beneficiary payments for this SPIA, the entire remaining $45,000 SPIA purchase cost gets to be tax deducted as a loss in the father's estate on the final income tax return in the same manner as above.

Beneficiary Claims

When SPIA annuitants die, it is imperative family members or other beneficiaries notify the insurance company as soon as possible. SPIA contracts with life-contingent payments are only legally bound to make payments while the annuitants are alive. However, if the SPIA payment is due on the fifteenth of the month and the annuitant dies on the fourteenth, it may not be administratively possible to report the death claim and stop the payment prior to its regular date. With the advent of electronic banking, such payments will inevitably be made. Depending on the wording in the SPIA contract, most carriers count someone being alive as of 12:01 a.m. on the payment date as being eligible for the payment. In fact, family members sometimes do not report the annuitant's death to the insurance company for several months and collect annuity overpayments.

Many times, this is simply because the family didn't know Mom or Dad owned a SPIA. The annuity company eventually seeks a return of these payments, often with additional interest in the annual range of 6 to 7 percent. The rate applied to overpayment collections is usually stated in the SPIA contract. Abusive situations, where many months lapse between the annuitant's date of death and the reporting date, can bring a formal debt collection action under "unjust enrichment" litigation.

This problem also applies to period-certain-only beneficiaries. After the date of annuitant death, the annuitant's estate is not entitled to continue receiving period-certain annuity payments; the carrier is responsible for making those payments to contract beneficiaries. If there is an overpayment to the annuitant's estate, the carrier has to re-collect these payments to make up for what they paid the contract beneficiaries once they were notified of the death claim.

Carriers constantly perform searches of the "Death Master File" maintained by the Social Security Administration for unreported annuitant deaths. Typically, the carrier catches an unreported death within a few months by cross-referencing the Social Security numbers in its records. This helps mitigate carrier SPIA overpayments (and/or paying the wrong individuals).

Beneficiaries Who Inherit SPIA Rights

While deferred annuities and life insurance are not covered in this book, aspects of deferred annuities and life insurance that relate to immediate annuities are covered. *Beneficiaries of deferred annuity contracts and life insurance policies receive the same rights and guarantees their former owners had unless, the contract states otherwise.* Beneficiaries also receive the same tax benefits. This is critical, as it pertains to annuity options or annuity settlement options, which are immediate annuity provisions found in all deferred annuity contracts and life insurance policies.

In other words, rather than take the lump-sum death benefit of the deferred annuity or life insurance policy, it may behoove beneficiaries to review the settlement or annuity options they are eligible to receive. Many older deferred annuity contracts and life insurance policies held by parents have very high guaranteed interest rates and very old mortality tables versus the newer contracts that are far less generous in both regards. The higher the guaranteed interest rate and the older the mortality table (unadjusted), the higher the annuity income rate available to contract beneficiaries versus current market rates. In addition, the deferred annuity cost basis accrues to the beneficiary. For life insurance, the life insurance face amount becomes the immediate annuity cost basis. *Depending on this cost basis and the annuity elected, only some or none of the annuity income may be taxable.*

If your father dies and you are a male who inherits his contract or policy at age sixty-five with a 5.50 percent guaranteed interest rate, and the carrier guarantees the use of the 1971 Individual Annuity Mortality Table, your monthly income per thousand of cash value is $7.36 for an immediate annuity paid on your life for ten years period certain and your lifetime thereafter. This equates to $736 per month for every $100,000 inherited. However, because annuity interest rates are so low today and carriers keep adjusting for longer life expectancies, the same annuity purchased for the same premium cost today only produces $531 of monthly income—about 28 percent less!

Beneficiaries can reap huge financial rewards just by inheriting deferred annuity contracts or life insurance policies with their higher guaranteed rates and compelling the insurance company to convert all or a portion of the deferred annuity or life insurance policy into an income immediate annuity for themselves.

The beneficiary's nontaxable income portion is determined by the same IRS tables the former owner would have used and is based on the annuity the beneficiary elects and the cost basis in the annuity contract. For example, if instead the beneficiary elected a ten-year period-certain annuity paid for 120 months, the monthly income would be $1,074. This equates to a total guaranteed income of $128,880. At current rates, a carrier would only have to pay about $895 per month, or $107,400, of total guaranteed income—about 17 percent less.

If the deferred annuity contract's tax basis was $128,880 ($28,880 more than the cash value), none of the ten-year period-certain income is taxable to the beneficiary! This could have occurred because the parent suffered some irreversible losses in the deferred contract or perhaps transferred it via a 1035 transaction to exchange funds from a life insurance policy or another annuity contract that had also lost money, and the parent never had a chance of recovering these losses prior to his or her death. This is why it's really important for consumers to review inherited deferred annuity contracts or life insurance death claims with professional annuity agents prior to making a death claim settlement election with the parent's annuity or life insurance carrier.

The number-one tip is this: don't expect the insurance company to blatantly point out the richness of their SPIA guaranteed rates found in their deferred annuity contracts or life insurance policies.

Consumers should never settle a death claim prior to seeing a copy of the annuity contract or the life insurance policy. If you can't find your parent's deferred annuity contract or life insurance policy, order one from the carrier and review it prior to signing off on the death claim settlement. The agent can review available immediate annuity options guaranteed by the parent's contract simultaneously with the deferred annuity's tax status to help determine the best course of action for the deferred annuity beneficiary.

In this super-low interest rate environment, you may find your deceased parent's deferred annuity contract or life insurance policy rescuing your own retirement income needs.

Generally, for deferred annuity contracts and life insurance policies issued after 2008, many carriers lowered their guarantees regarding annuity options or annuity settlement rates to better reflect poor economic times.

Beneficiaries Who Are Irrevocable
Beneficiary changes are an owner's right. This is important because the owner may wish to change the beneficiary(s) sometime after the SPIA contract is purchased. While there are all kinds of beneficiary designations for gift tax purposes, they have impacts if they are made "irrevocable." I'm not going to discuss gift taxes because they are tied into estate taxation, which is another book. Basically when a SPIA beneficiary is made irrevocable, the owner is making a gift of the present value of the property. This value may have current gift tax implications for individuals with larger multi-million dollar estates.

Joint Annuitants Who Become Owners
Joint and survivor annuitant SPIAs are treated a little differently. If the surviving annuitant becomes the new owner the

remaining payments and cost basis transfer to them also. They receive taxable income in the same manner as the former annuitant and owner. If the surviving annuitant dies prior to receiving the entire cost basis, then the tax deduction for lost insurance premium is taken in the survivor's estate.

SPIA Changes (Post Issue)

SPIAs for the most part are not flexible; this is good for safety issues (see "Protection" chapter) but can be detrimental for other needs. Some SPIA contracts contain language that permits owner latitude to make changes after the contract is issued by the insurance company. The main areas are; payment reductions for an optional lump-sum payment (if offered), advanced payments (if offered), ownership and beneficiary changes and bank changes for crediting receipt of income.

Payment Changes

A few SPIA contracts, predominantly nonqualified contracts, have payment commutation or withdrawal features, and the direct financial costs of these features are disclosed in the contract. The purpose of this feature is to convert future scheduled payments into a lump sum sometime after the SPIA contract is issued. Just how often this can be elected and what payments are subject to this election depend on the SPIA contract.

While some carriers and agents believe this makes the SPIA more attractive to purchasing consumers, it does so at a cost. The safety benefit one receives for purchasing the SPIA in the first place is diminished (see "Protection" chapter), and there is some uncertainty about how the IRS might view the surviving SPIA contract post the commutation or withdrawal request.

First let's look at the taxation of the commutation or withdrawal amount itself. This is important because it is different from how a withdrawal amount is taxed from a deferred annuity under the last-in first-out (LIFO) rule and fully taxable. For SPIA payment commutations or withdrawals, the pro rata rule is used. In other words, for income tax purposes, part of the SPIA lump-sum amount is treated as a withdrawal of the SPIA cost basis, and part of the withdrawal is taxable.

In the case of a SPIA payment commutation or withdrawal, the insurance company will calculate how much of the withdrawal is attributed to what element (the cost basis vs. the contract gains). For example, if you withdraw $20,000 as a lump sum from your SPIA because you commuted some of future scheduled payments, $15,000 of this amount may not be taxable because this was the amount attributable to cost basis at the time of withdrawal. In this case, $5,000 ($20,000 - $15,000) is taxable.

For partial SPIA commutations or withdrawals, the remaining contract payments decrease and the nontaxable amount is recalculated. This is where a potential tax problem lies. The IRS defines SPIAs as contracts that feature "annually and substantially equal payments." This is referred to as the "substantially equal payment" doctrine. SPIA payments that don't conform to this rule may cause the contract to lose SPIA tax treatment. Since the IRS has never opined on what "substantially equal" means, it causes some tax treatment uncertainty. In this light, let's look at SPIA contract variability.

Period-certain payment only contracts are a little easier for all concerned, and typically the entire period-certain payment can be entirely or even partially commuted and withdrawn. In this case, I might have a ten-year (120 month) contract featuring an $890 monthly payment. If, after two years, with eight remaining payment years, I decide to commute 50 percent of this payment, the payment reduces to $445 ($890 – 50 percent or $445). The withdrawal is $42,720 ($445 x 12 x 8), assuming no expenses.

However what about the IRS "substantially equal payment" rule? Is the $890 payment substantially equal to the $445 remaining payment? Not really. But this is how most SPIA payment commutations affect the remaining payments.

Some carriers a little more sensitive to this tax issue do SPIA commutations differently. For period-certain-only contracts, they do not adjust the payment. Using the above example rather than reducing the payment to $445, these carries reduce the payment duration.

If the above SPIA has eight remaining payment years at the time of the request, paying a monthly rate of $890, and to arrive at the same $42,720 withdrawal, the carrier reduces the remaining payment by four years ($890 x 12 x 4), leaving four years in the contract from the remaining eight years at the time of the request. This way the IRS can't challenge the contract under the substantially equal payment doctrine because the monthly payment remains at $890.

Period-certain and life contracts are more problematic. This is a mixed-priced contract; some part of the contract pricing is based on interest rates and some part of the SPIA pricing is based on annuitant "mortality" (see "Variability" chapter). One of the quandaries the carrier faces is a pricing benefit was given to the consumer when he or she purchased the mortality-based SPIA in the form of higher payments attributable to the annuitant's chance of death (see "Variability" chapter). Later on, well after the contract was issued to permit annuitants to make withdrawals in the light of declining heath circumstances, the carrier is placed at risk from a phenomenon known as "adverse selection." If it becomes rampant, carriers can be significantly, financially damaged by adverse selection.

In other words, a bargain was struck between the annuitant and the insurance company for higher payments in exchange for the payments being life contingent. Then, well after the SPIA contract is issued, to let consumers out of the bargain merely because of an adverse health change can be costly for the insurance company. Because of this, typically only period-certain only payments can be commuted.

For example, if I purchased a twenty-year period-certain and lifetime thereafter contract, after five years I could elect to commute all or part of the remaining fifteen period-certain years. Typically the life-contingent years cannot be commuted. If my initial monthly payment is $500, it might become $350 or even $0 for the next fifteen years in exchange for a lump sum now. If the SPIA contract permits several lump-sum elections, the payment might become $350, and then $250, and then $0, depending on how many lump-sum elections I'm permitted to make. However, after fifteen years, if I survive, the life-contingent payments kick in at the initial $500 monthly rate. So are these payments "annually" and "substantially equal"? Not really.

Certain and lifetime thereafter contracts can't reduce the payment duration like period-certain-only contracts because they are, well, by definition, lifetime payment contracts.

Because of this tax quandary, a few carriers actually permit a reduction of both period-certain and life-contingent payments. The way they protect themselves with annuity pricing and conform better to the IRS annually and substantially equally payment doctrine is they limit payment commutation to no more than one request over the life of the contract, and they limit the payment change to no more than 10 percent. This way only a small part of the life-contingent payment and the period-certain portion can be removed. The payment reduction limit of 10 percent makes it harder for the IRS to make a case the annuity payments going forward are not substantially equal. In other words, if my initial monthly annuity payment is $1,000, and now, after commutation, it is $900 (10 percent less) it's hard for the IRS to argue $900 is not substantially equal to $1,000.

Another more clever way some SPIA carriers have adapted to this IRS tax uncertainty is via a SPIA payment advance. Instead of altering the SPIA payment, the carrier just advances six payments upon request. For example, if my monthly payment is $1,000 in December, I might request a six payment advance starting in January. In this case, the carrier gives me a lump-sum check for $6,000 in January and my next scheduled $1,000 monthly payment starts again in July. The payments remained unchanged and some liquidity is offered by the carrier, and the SPIA contract might permit several payment advance requests over the life of the contract.

Ownership Changes
Another very big benefit of the SPIA contract is the ability for the owner to change the contract ownership to a new owner. Not all SPIA contracts offer this property right, but it can be a very desirable feature—particularly if the owner wants or needs to gift the property to a son or daughter, sibling, or a trust. One of the income tax benefits of making such a gift is the income tax reporting now goes to the new owner, who receives all the income.

Unlike a deferred annuity, where such a gift would cause the current owner a taxable income to the extent of contract gains at the time of the gift, a SPIA contracts shares none of this problem. A deferred annuity is considered an "un-matured" contract, and as such, if I as the owner have a taxable gain of ten thousand dollars when I give the contract to anyone (not a spouse) or any entity except for certain trusts, I have to pay the tax on this gain immediately.

However, if I give a SPIA, which is considered by the IRS to be a "fully matured contract," that contains gains, I do not need to recognize a gain. There is no more income tax deferral, and the new Owner starts to pay income tax on the taxable portion of the SPIA income.

For example; if I purchase a fifteen-year period certain-only contract with a monthly payment of $321 for a premium cost of $50,000, my deferred gain is $7,780 ($321 x 180) – $50,000 purchase cost. If I use the proceeds of a former deferred annuity or life insurance policy to purchase my SPIA and that annuity or policy itself had a gain of $10,000, then that gain is also carried over under the 1035 exchange rules. In this case, my total deferred gain is $17,780 ($7,780 + $10,000 deferred gain).

If, I'm sixty years old and I purchase a fifteen-year period certain and lifetime SPIA, my gain is not so easily determined. Perhaps I purchase a Joint and Survivor SPIA. The gain for this is not so easily determined either. Does the gain conclude at the end of a certain period or at the end of some single or joint life expectancy table? Furthermore, which table would be used? There are several tables.

This distinction is important because, generally, income earned by one person normally can't be shifted to another for income tax purposes under the IRS fruit-of-the-tree doctrine. SPIAs seem to be the one exception. For the IRS to address this exception, it would not only have to change the tax code language but also determine how to calculate the gain.

This technique only addresses income tax issues and not possible gift tax issues, which may be more complicated depending on the givers' estate value and the value of the gift. We will not go into gift taxes here.

Entity Ownership
If permitted by the SPIA contract, the SPIA could be owned by an entity. This entity could be a business or perhaps a personal trust, such as a living trust. This type of ownership is usually for property control purposes. These entities might have more elaborate ownership control provisions that a simple SPIA individual ownership can't directly provide for. For example, if the business owner or trustee becomes incapacitated, then a successor control person would be named in such an event. Normally, entities don't receive annuity taxable income deferrals. Similarly, a corporate entity does not receive income tax deferrals on contract gains in a deferred annuity (cash-value) contract. For a cash-value deferred annuity, the corporation receives a yearly 1099 for the earned interest.

Because they don't have cash values, SPIAs and deferred income annuities (DIAs) are exceptions to the general annuity rule regarding contract gains when contracts are owned by entities.

For example: A corporation purchases a deferred income annuity on the owner or key employee's life as the annuitant. The owner or employee is fifty years old, and the DIA initial payment starts at the annuitant's age sixty-five, and is then paid for lifetime only. The premium cost is $50,000, and assuming a female annuitant, the monthly income is $555 or $6,660 yearly. Using the IRS table V for life expectancy determination (twenty years), in this case, the deferred expected gain is: $83,320 ($6,660 x 20 years – $50,000 annuity purchase cost). Of course the gain could exceed this amount if the annuitant continued to survive.

Assuming corporate contract ownership, none of this gain becomes taxable income to the corporate owner, until payments begin in fifteen years at the annuitant's age sixty-five. At this time if the DIA permitted an owner change, the contract could then just be transferred to the retiring employee or owner, who as the new owner would be responsible for the income taxes on the income. Normally, as a premium cost recovery, about 37 percent of the annual income is not taxable for twenty years. If the annuitant survives to the age of eighty-five, the DIA income becomes 100 percent taxable. In this case, this is of course dependent upon the tax categorization of the annuity transfer to the employee.

Qualified Purchase Premium
The importance of cost basis is not relevant for qualified SPIA contracts, because none of the funds in a "qualified" plan such as a pension, 401(k) or most traditional IRAs have been taxed yet. All payments from SPIAs purchased with qualified funds derived from such retirement plans are taxable as "ordinary income" at the individual tax rates.

IRS Required Minimum Distributions (RMDs)
However, the IRS does intervene. They want individuals who purchase qualified SPIAs to significantly benefit from

these contracts and not their beneficiaries. There are certain SPIA payments that work to reduce the SPIA's current income, trading it off for higher income at later dates. Under the IRS required minimum distribution (RMD) rules that affect all IRAs and pensions and other qualified retirement plans, SPIAs that are IRAs or are otherwise "qualified" are also affected by the RMD rules

SPIAs that pay reduced payments versus a single-life payment are contracts that contain period-certain, joint and survivor annuitants and cost of living adjustments because these kinds of SPIA provisions are really "incidental" to a payment for just a single life provision. After 2006, SPIA incidental benefits must be accounted for in the IRS math for RMD compliance.

The reason for this is incidental benefits reduced SPIA payments when compared to just a single life without incidental benefits.

While you are permitted to have some incidental benefits to provide for your beneficiaries, that the IRS deems are reasonable legacy benefits, you can't just load the SPIA contract up with incidental benefit provisions and effectively pass most of your intended benefits on to your beneficiaries.

The good news is all the annuity carriers know what these limits are and, by now, have likely modified their systems to make sure a non-RMD compliant SPIA does not get issued. Whatever the SPIA income is, as long as the incidental benefit requirement is met, the SPIA income will automatically be compliant for IRS RMD purposes. The income from the SPIA only works for that SPIA and cannot be used to offset IRS RMD requirements for other IRAs you may also own.

Let's see how this works for a male, age seventy-five, who is purchasing a $50,000 SPIA with a monthly payment starting thirty days after the purchase date, in a few different scenarios to illustrate the incidental benefit impact on the monthly payment (see table below).

Annuity Incidental Benefits

Annuity	Monthly Payment	Annual Income**
Life-only	$359	$4,308
10-Years Certain & Life	$319	$3,828
10 – Year Certain & Life with 3% Cost of Living Adjustment	$285	$3,420
Joint 100% Survivor Annuity with Female Spouse Age 70	$254	$3,048
Joint 100% Survivor Annuity with Son Age 50	$190	$2,280

**Monthly income x 12

As you can see, the annual income diminishes when you start to add incidental benefits on a SPIA contract versus a life-only payment. The reason for this is the carrier needs to reduce the initial life-only payment to conserve annuity value because the carrier might be required to make additional payments to contract beneficiaries or other annuitants when the SPIA IRA contract holder dies. This is done by creating an internal deferral.

While the first four annuity purchase scenarios in the table above are available for qualified SPIA contracts, the last one—the joint 100 percent survivor annuity with son age fifty is not. In this purchase scenario, the monthly payment of $190 is ultra-low when compared to the life-only payment of $359.

The payment is ultra-low because the son is only age fifty, and although the father is seventy-five, the insurance company has to reduce the monthly payment to make sure there are sufficient funds to pay the much-younger son over his lifetime when the father dies. The IRS has a problem with this because the internal deferral to the son is too great at the expense of the father's current income.

In this case, due to the father-son age difference, the IRS says upon the father's death, the benefit to his son must be reduced to no more than 66 percent of the father's amount. There is an IRS table for this situation.

Upon the father's death, because the son now receives less than 100 percent of the father's payment, there is more money to pay the father, and his initial monthly income rises to $230 from the original $190. In this case, when the father dies, the son receives $152 ($230 x 66 percent) per month for as long as the son survives. If the son dies before the —father—something that isn't too likely but could —happen—then the father continues to receive the $230 monthly income until he dies.

In this manner, the IRS controls the total annual incomes permitted under the RMD rules for qualified money SPIA purchases.

In the other cases, if the period-certain duration is too long, say twenty-five or thirty years, this might have to be reduced to twenty years maximum. If the applied-for COLA is 5 to 6 percent, this might have to be reduced to 2 to 3 percent maximum. The insurance carrier is responsible for making sure the SPIA contracts they issue are going to pass muster with the IRS under the RMD rules. But just to make sure, consumers should have their agents verify with their carriers that the proper SPIAs are being issued—which is another excellent reason for dealing with a knowledgeable SPIA agent.

Note

*Withdrawals from deferred annuity contracts that contain premiums (cash), paid prior to August 14, 1982, are taxed after all the premium costs are withdrawn first under the "first-in, first-out" (FIFO) rule. None of the withdrawals from these contracts for this premium are taxable until the entire premium cost is withdrawn, and any withdrawals from gains are taxed last. This is an important deferred annuity income tax benefit and can carry forward to future deferred annuity contracts following 1035 exchange activity.

Chapter Summary

• The tax benefits of SPIA ownership are second only to safety as a reason to purchase. Such benefits accrue to the owner(s) and, depending on the contract, any beneficiary who becomes a new contract owner.

• For income tax purposes, SPIA contracts are classified as nonqualified (if purchased with after-tax funds) and qualified (if purchased with pretax funds).

• Nonqualified contracts have a "cost basis" (usually the purchase cost of the contract). In the case of exchange/ replacement transactions, this cost basis transfers over from the former annuity contract or life insurance policy. The nontaxable portion of the cost basis is returned to the contract owner over the duration of the annuity or over the life expectancy table the IRS deems necessary, depending on the contract.

• SPIA beneficiaries, depending on the contract, also receive tax benefits. Beneficiaries have certain responsibilities to submit timely notices of annuitant death, and beneficiaries of deferred annuity contracts and life insurance policies inherit SPIA rights along with all the same contract guarantees of the former owners unless, the contract or policy states otherwise.

• Some SPIA contracts permit payment changes as a consequence of contract withdrawals or payment commutations. Aggressive withdrawals may result in adverse income tax treatment of the remaining SPIA payments.

• Some SPIA contracts permit ownership changes and entity ownership with favorable income tax treatments.

• Because none of the funds in a qualified SPIA have been taxed, such contracts don't have a cost basis that is returned nontaxable to the contract owner. Due to required minimum distribution (RMD) requirements and "incidental" contract provisions, federal rules still dictate the kind of qualified SPIAs individuals can purchase.

AGENT

"Act well your part; there all the honor lies"
—Alexander Pope, English poet

**"If you keep faith with people and tell them
the truth even when it threatens their beliefs,
you run the risk of losing them. But if you
pedal cleverly manipulated talking points to
people who trust you not to lie, you won't
merely lose them; you'll break their hearts"**

—Unknown

Introduction
The annuity agent is really a life insurance agent because there isn't a separate state insurance license for annuity agents. Typically, an agent must complete approximately forty hours of classroom instruction and take a written state insurance exam, pay initial and annual state fees, and be appointed (authorized to sell on the behalf of an insurance company) to an insurance company in his or her resident state. The agent may also maintain other nonresident state insurance licenses. As a matter of practice, a good agent will always carry a copy of his or her state insurance licenses just in case a consumer requests to see a copy. Consumers, as a matter of protection and prior to doing business with an agent, you might want to make a habit of requesting such a copy.

No matter what you might have heard to the contrary, the annuity agent is primarily compensated by commission, which is paid on the annuity contracts he or she sells for the insurance carriers the agent represents. Some agents may represent only one carrier, while other agents may represent several. Although there are a few agents who might work on a fee basis, these individuals are few and far between. Being compensated on commission for paid sales creates a dynamic for the selling agent. Home office personnel are salaried employees of the insurance company who labor behind the scenes and work with agents to place businesses and manage the insurance company's affairs.

For the most part, agents are pretty resourceful and good-natured individuals. A good agent can usually find a way to get you what you need. I often tell the following story about agents and employees at their home office.

Agent Story
The story goes like this: the president of the insurance company orders his top agency manager, and his five agents, the home office new business manager, and five department employees each to travel by train from New York to Atlanta for a week-long insurance conference. The purpose of the long train trip was to create much needed camaraderie between these two departments in order to set aside some longstanding differences.

Both managers grumbled, but, in the end, were compelled by an executive order to travel together, stay in the same hotel and attend the conference.

However, at the New York train station, competitive spirits emerged. The new business manager was the first one in line and ordered tickets for himself and his entire staff. After seeing this, the agency manager stepped up to the ticket window and said, "One ticket, please." The ticket clerk punched out one ticket. Seeing this, the new business manager said, "I would like to see how you are going to get you and your entire staff to Atlanta with just one ticket." All the new business department employees laughed, but, the agents remained silent.

After they were on the train and bound for Atlanta, the train conductor entered their train car and began to collect tickets. At the sight of the conductor, all the agents got up, ran to a bathroom stall and piled in on top of the agency manager, who was sitting on the toilet with the door closed.

As the conductor only saw the agency manager's legs in the stall, he merely knocked on the door and said, "Ticket please." Out slid the single ticket. After the conductor left the train car for the next one, the agents piled out of the stall, rolling with laughter after realizing they've gotten the best of the home office employees.

Now seething, the home office employees determined to get the agents back at the end of the week during the return trip to New York.

At the Atlanta train station upon the return trip, the new business department manager stepped up to the ticket window and smugly ordered only one ticket. "Two can play at this game," he said. The agency manager seeing this, stepped up to the ticket window, visibly hesitated, and walked away without ordering a single ticket!

At this point, all the home office employees were incredulous at the temerity of the agency manager, thinking he was going to get himself and his entire staff to New York with no tickets. Laughing to themselves, the home office employees assumed all the agents were definitely going to get their butts kicked off the train at the first stop.

When the train departed for New York, the train conductor again entered the car to collect tickets. At the sight of the conductor, all the home office employees rushed to the bathroom, piled into a stall, closed the door, assumed the position, and snickered while waiting for the conductor. After a minute went by, the agency manager calmly rose from his seat, knocked on the bathroom stall door and said, "ticket please."

Role

Agents, the primary distributors of insurance carriers' products, are constantly on the lookout for potential clients or those who might introduce them to potential clients who may benefit from an annuity contract. There needs to be a real level of trust established between the agent and the consumer for a transaction to occur. An agent can't buy trust; it has to be earned. In general, to some degree, insurance is viewed as a necessary evil by the consuming public. Insurance policies and annuities are no exceptions. They use opaque legal language; the marketing literature isn't necessarily all that clear; and many times, an agent can be viewed as the adversary. It becomes a difficult task for the consumer to determine if he or she is getting a "deal."

It isn't easy for the annuity agent either. Annuity contracts are an intangible item. Other than the paper they are written on, there is nothing for the consumer to touch and feel to get excited about. For the agent, it isn't like those home property shows on television where the couple just ooh's and ah's over a beautiful home renovation and cries and profusely thanks the realtor or home builder for the beautiful work he or she just accomplished on the remodel job.

Although the life insurance industry (annuity industry) is considerably more professional today, that wasn't always the case. Just after the turn of the twentieth century, the industry went through a major scandal in 1905. The Governor of New York, Frank W. Higgins, called for a political committee to investigate certain corrupt business practices of the insurance industry. Known as the Armstrong Committee, it revealed questionable insurance business dealings and by the time 1905 concluded, the insurance industry lost creditability. Scandals also popped up in the 1970s and 1980s, and then there was a big problem: a few life insurance companies issuing annuity contracts went out of business. Even today, annuity carriers' failures haunt the industry and can damage agent reputations.

For the annuity agents, there are no public adulations; they are not publically celebrated, and there are no hallowed halls an agent can traverse—except, of course, when something goes terribly wrong for the consumer. Then, miraculously, consumer attitudes change. This becomes somewhat analogous to individuals who are critical of their country but, in times of war, look tentatively over their shoulders just to make sure Old Glory is still flying.

As in everything else, you have some highly trained individuals with lots of experience and others who are poorly trained with little experience. Just like in other industries, you also find a few unscrupulous individuals. For the most part, however, you will find the average agent is really a caring soul who wants to satisfy his or her clients but is also aware he or she may be the deliverer of bad news. Sometimes a good agent has to be able to give tough love.

Agents sit on consumers' shoulders, whispering in their ears that something could go terribly wrong and reminding consumers their worlds may not always be so rosy. Sometimes it can be a tough job being an annuity or SPIA agent. But sometimes, as a SPIA agent, you get to put a stake in the heart of the bad guy. That's most satisfying indeed (see "Protection" chapter, "Marital Property" chapter, and "Anecdotes").

The states have taken recent measures to make sure annuity agents have more training from the companies and in annuity products they represent. The states have imposed new general annuity continuing education requirements. States require annuity agents to take at least four continuing education (CE) credit hours of general annuity training to maintain agent licensing, and some states make this an annual requirement upon each future insurance license renewal. Overall agents must take between fifteen and twenty five credit hours every couple of years. Companies must show state regulators their agents receive annuity specific training in the products they represent. So, annuity training is on the rise.

Some annuity agents also have supplemental formal training and education. This training and education, while not annuity specific, is represented by designations such as certified financial planner (CFP©), chartered life underwriter (CLU©), and chartered financial consultant (ChFC©). This supplemental training takes several years to complete and speaks to the agent's overall insurance industry training and personal financial expertise.

Insurance carriers now have entire departments dedicated to annuity application reviews. Each annuity application is reviewed prior to the contract placed date for consumer purchase suitability issues. In the opinion of the annuity carrier, if the supporting consumer disclosure documents that arrive with the annuity application don't support the transaction for a particular consumer, the annuity application is turned back or the carrier's accepted premium is reduced.

In addition to the annuity carrier, if the annuity agent is employed by a commercial bank or a securities brokerage firm, these organizations also conduct their own initial annuity application review procedures that also vet annuity applications prior to the carrier review. In a huge consumer protection intervention movement, recent regulations over the last five to six years established annuity purchase suitability review hurdles. The annuity agent now has to work more carefully with many reviewers who have differing opinions to establish a good case for consumer annuity purchase suitability.

Annuity agents also sign lengthy selling agreements with their respective carriers. These selling agreements cover the scope of the agents' authority, obligations, what they can and cannot do while selling the carriers products, financial repercussions, and burdens for violating the agreement.

But how does this relate particularly to SPIAs? SPIAs still maintain the distinction of the smallest market share of all the retail annuity lines. If you add all the commercial SPIAs, structured settlement contracts, and charitable contracts together, you just might exceed sales of $15 billion per year; but fixed and variable deferred annuity contracts sales total $100 billion plus per year.

Although there are various reasons for the above sales differences—some of which are driven by consumer demographics—there are also very substantial reasons that have to do with how agents are compensated. Typically, a SPIA agent might earn a sales commission of anywhere from 2.50 to 4.00 percent on the paid premium, depending on the contract, where a deferred annuity sales agent might earn a commission of anywhere from 4.00 to 8.00 percent on the paid premium, depending on the contract and the

annuitant's or Owner's age. Generally, for deferred annuities, the higher the age the lower the commission.

If you were an agent working strictly on commission,
you would spend more of your time locating appropriate
consumers for deferred annuity contracts than for SPIA
contracts because deferred annuity contracts pay you more
commission income. However, the deferred annuity agent
is exposed to some post-sale financial risks. Typically,
if the annuitant or the owner depending on the contract
dies during the first year, the agent has to return all or part
of his or her commission to the company (a commission
charge-back). Also, some carriers have started to impose a
commission "charge-back" on their agents if the consumer
exercises deferred annuity contract income options.

There are typically no agent commission charge-backs
for SPIA contracts unless, for some reason, the contract is
returned by the owner to the carrier for a premium refund.

In almost all cases, annuity commissions are not
disclosed to consumers except in New York state under
regulation 194. Under this regulation, when an application
is taken, the consumer receives a notice from the agent.
The notice informs the consumer of his or her right to seek
a written commission disclosure from the agent's company.
The consumer's written inquiry must be received by the
annuity company within thirty days of the application date or
within thirty days following the contract issue date.

Besides the compensation issue that reflects the above
differences, there is also a training issue that has its roots in
the historical development of today's annuity agents. SPIAs'
immediate income or deferred income contracts were the
predominate contracts sold to consumers until about the
late 1970s and the very early 1980s when the annuity industry went through a structural change. This had to do with

the deregulation movement that effected financial services companies.

Up until that time, life insurance agents primarily sold other lines, such as life insurance, disability and health insurance. Very few agents actually sold annuity contracts because annuity commissions were tremendously lower than the other lines, and agents were more accustomed to selling insurance policies that were funded by monthly or annual premium payments.

However, at that time interest rates were also going through the roof. Remember the early 1980s? Consumers were striping out life insurance policy cash values or just sur-rendering their life insurance policies outright and reinvesting the proceeds into higher yielding money market accounts and the growing mutual fund industry products to try to achieve better returns. Some insurance carriers developed "term life" insurance coverage. Term life insurance is an inexpensive life insurance policy relative to the traditional whole life insur-ance policy, with its large cash values that was predominantly sold at the time. Many financial advisors started selling this low-cost life insurance coverage hand in hand with invest-ment products like mutual funds and money market accounts. Other carriers developed universal life insurance, a policy with tremendous flexibility, cash values, and the ability to credit current interest rates as the market changed.

The life insurance industry was bleeding cash and had to come up with a way to offer attractive consumer returns to compete with the other financial service competitors. This is how the "modern" single premium deferred annuity was created. First there was fixed-interest bearing products; then, later, annuity contracts were melded with mutual funds to create variable deferred annuities. In more recent years, fixed indexed deferred annuities were created, and hybrid deferred annuities melded with long-term care benefits and other features.

However, if life insurance agents who were only used to selling SPIAs sold an annuity at all, they weren't too comfortable with this new turn of events. The life insurance industry, facing agent sales opposition, turned to stockbrokers of major firms like Merrill Lynch and Dean Witter, etc. to sell the new deferred annuities. While stockbrokers in general, were better trained to gather assets for investment purposes than the insurance agents of the era, there was some initial stockbroker resistance. This resistance melted when fixed deferred annuity contracts started to credit 14 to 15 percent guaranteed annual interest rates to reflect the current rates of the early 1980s.

So it began—the fall of the SPIA and the rise of the deferred annuity. When the deregulation environment hit the major stockbrokerage firms and stockbrokerage commissions were deregulated, many of the big firms reduced their sales forces. These brokers left the major firms in droves and started their own firms or reestablished themselves in the fledging broker-dealer community. Guess what? They took their annuity clients and all their deferred annuity training with them. So, for thirty years, the deferred annuity market grew in leaps in bounds. In fact, 1982 was the first year new annuity premiums from all sources exceeded new life insurance premiums since the Great Depression era from 1934 to 1936. Then, in 1993, annuity premiums from individual annuity sales alone exceeded all life premiums and the annuity industry never looked back. Now annuity premiums dominate life premiums and they have for several decades.

But if the deferred annuity industry grew leaps and bounds, what became of the SPIA industry? It stagnated considerably over this same time. SPIA agents retired, some died, and SPIA training waned. There was little to no SPIA product development relative to the deferred annuity world; carriers became uninterested in placing SPIA business and went after the more lucrative deferred annuity business. In fact, only a couple of carriers successfully introduced truly unique mortality-based SPIA contract structures over the last thirty years. Most SPIA contract structures on the market today are a holdover from the turn of the twentieth century.

Many agents concentrated on the deferred annuity world during this time. Consumer demographics also supported the sales of deferred annuities to younger consumers trying to accumulate retirement funds. For roughly thirty years until about 2008, agents purchased new deferred contracts for their clients and exchanged old annuity contracts and life insurance for new deferred annuity contracts. So, in this manner, annuity agents created and managed an entire retail client "book" of annuity business over this time. A retail client book might be $50–$100 million or more of retail deferred annuity contract cash values and perhaps spread over a client population of five hundred individuals or more.

When interest rates collapsed in 2008, annuity agents found it difficult to offer new interest crediting deferred contracts to their clients either through new cash purchases or annuity contract exchanges. Interest rates on deferred annuity contracts sank to about 2.00 percent and, considering the average, interest-bearing deferred annuity contracts required five to seven years of surrender charges. Consumers shunned these ultra-low rates for new money purchases. Older interest-bearing fixed deferred annuity contracts issued prior to and at the turn of the twenty-first century had such great guaranteed interest rates (rates way above the current market) and other provisions agents found it difficult to improve on their clients' annuity contract positions; annuity exchange activity also dried up. For the last ten years or so, the fixed deferred annuity world has given rise to the fixed indexed annuity (FIA). While this particular deferred annuity also credits interest, it does so through complex indexing formulas.

Also during this time, variable deferred annuities ran into all kinds of problems. Although, at the time of this writing, fixed indexed annuities are still doing well with sales, they have other regulatory issues and may face similar challenges that variable annuities are currently facing today.

Primarily, many of these challenges arise out of the growth of complexity of the modern deferred variable annuity and fixed index deferred annuity contracts. In fact, these contracts have become so complex both consumers and agents struggle with the contracts' terms and conditions. Contracts have grown in physical size from six to seven pages for the average interest bearing deferred annuity contract to forty pages or more for the average variable deferred annuity and fixed index deferred annuity contracts. The marketing literature and disclosures have also increased in size. As these contracts become more complex, it becomes quite challenging for many annuity agents to competently sell and explain to their clients the deferred annuity contracts they are representing today.

This complexity eventually led to all kinds of consumer agent complaints to state regulators and swarms of civil law suits regarding the sales of deferred annuity contracts. The states eventually cracked down by increasing agent training requirements. Many carriers reached financial settlements with consumer groups. Today, the deferred annuity landscape is much different than what existed at the turn of the twenty-first century. The current and persistent, repressive interest rate environment continues to dictate deferred annuity contract changes, agent compensation and annuity industry players.

In the years since 2008, and something that caught annuity agents by surprise, was the support of SPIAs by what I call "the ivory tower" types—all the economists, pension experts, "celebrity" actuaries, and so on—who constantly publish articles in prestigious trade journals, major national newspapers, and online websites, extolling their virtues. While the rest of the annuity industry was struggling to regain its annuity footing, these individuals supported the SPIA marketplace and helped to drive a kind of SPIA renaissance. Also, demographically, and due to retirement income needs, consumer interest has just begun to shift from deferred annuity accumulation features to income features. With interest rates at low points, "mortality credits" that SPIAs featured since the dawn of finance (see "History" chapter) have become an important way of driving higher, guaranteed retirement incomes (see "Contract" chapter) in this low-interest-rate economy. Unsurprisingly, the SPIA market has held its own and is experiencing a growth spurt.

However, due to lack of SPIA agent training, and for other agent compensation reasons, agents prefer to represent the more-complex deferred annuity contracts with new "income riders" that guarantee a certain level of clients' annual income via contract withdrawals (see "Pretenders to the Throne" Chapter). This agent and client bias is a holdover from the decades of deferred annuity contract comfort.

So, while there is tremendous newfound support for the SPIA from all kinds of qualified corners, the reality is SPIAs still don't enjoy marketplace levels of deferred annuity contracts. Consequently, agent SPIA training is also lacking. This contributes to misconceptions about SPIAs and where a SPIA might fit in the personal financial market place.

Critical Agent Role
Agents play a critical role in suggesting appropriate SPIA variability relative to their clients' needs. After gathering annuitant information spanning from personal financial disclosures to family and health concerns, the SPIA agent needs to strike a balance between the annuitant's income needs compared to his or her legacy desires. While life-contingent SPIAs produce higher incomes than period-certain only SPIAs of the same duration, life-contingent SPIAs offer no legacy benefits. While higher client income is a primary SPIA goal, the secondary goal is usually a legacy desire, and the two competing goals are really never that far apart.

The typical legacy SPIA structure is period-certain, because when the annuitant dies, remaining, unpaid period-certain payments and or their cash lump sum equivalents, depending on the contract are paid to the SPIA beneficiary(s). But period-certain payments as designated beneficiary(s) benefits have their limitations. If the annuitant survives the period-certain duration, then dies, the contract terminates with no beneficiary value (see "Brokerage" chapter).

Another better legacy design is just to place the intended beneficiary as the joint annuitant on the contract, but this choice needs to be evaluated by the agent based on the annuitant's circumstances (see "Brokerage" chapter).

The agent also needs to evaluate the annuitant's cash liquidity needs. Because of how SPIA pricing works, contracts are inherently not liquid financial products. If too much premium cost is incurred, the annuitant may not have the necessary liquidity to comfortably meet cash needs. However, if too little SPIA cost is incurred, the annuitant may not have the necessary protection he or she needs going forward into his or her twilight years (see "Protection" chapter).

If no single SPIA contract's variability meets the annuitant's need, then it may be time for the agent to consider SPIA contract combinations. The ability of the SPIA agent to design variability combinations in order to meet annuitant needs helps to separate the professional SPIA agent from competitors (see "Brokerage" chapter).

So, the SPIA agent has a lot to do and a huge responsibility. SPIAs, unlike deferred annuity contracts or life insurance policies, are permanent contracts and typically can't be altered after they are issued by the carrier. The annuitant and perhaps his or her beneficiary(s) will own the contract until the day he or she dies or at least as long as the annuity duration. A SPIA is probably the last permanent product that will ever be manufactured by any financial services industry participant.

Chapter Summary

• State-licensed agents must complete state-mandated annuity continuing education (CE) training and receive company annuity product training. They are primarily compensated with commissions paid by the carriers calculated on the annuity contracts they sell.

• Most annuity contracts sold today are deferred annuities of various kinds with withdrawal guarantees. This is largely due to agents' historical comfort with the deferred annuity contract design and to compensation issues.

• The SPIA agent's role is critical in helping consumers evaluate SPIA pricing and contract differences. Because these contracts are, for the most part, not liquid and effectively become permanent after the free look period, consumers are wise to incorporate a skilled SPIA agent to help them determine appropriate variability and competitive pricing for that variability.

BROKERAGE

**"How far that little candle throws its beams!
So shines a good deed in a naughty world."**
—William Shakespeare, English playwright

Introduction

Brokerage is the business of arranging a contract between two parties. Of course, in our case, we are talking about SPIA contract brokerage via an annuity agent. Mastering this skill helps to separate mediocre from truly great annuity agents. While many agents may choose to place single contracts for simple solutions, there are times when multiple SPIAs are required to achieve the desired results. SPIA variability and carrier contract availability becomes the color palette with which the SPIA agents paint. Intricate mortality-pooled lacing forms the consumer safety net below consumers' financial trapezes. The emerging SPIA picture is determined by clients' inputs and the agents' experiences in painting a SPIA solution. Sometimes black-on-white will do, and other times a whole array of colors is needed. The agents' artistry is tested when you consider all the SPIA elements previously discussed—contract language, taxation, estate benefits consideration, pricing, etc.

The Illustration

Before we can get into painting Rembrandts and Picassos, we need to fully understand the SPIA illustration that the agent usually provides the client at the initial client meeting. This illustration is usually a multipage document the agent or the agent's home office prepares with the aid of a computer software program designed for this purpose. The state may or may not have reviewed the illustration system and its output. The illustration is an important document, as it contains all the data input the agent gathered from the client to produce the SPIA quote. If any part of this data is inputted incorrectly, then the quote will not be accurate and the agent will not be able to make comparisons between competing carriers for the same annuity.

The illustration is just a pricing aid. There are many reasons SPIA quotes vary from company to company, even if the data input is the same. For example, annuity features can vary from contract to contract. One carrier may offer a future payment commutation feature, while another carrier may pay higher SPIA agent commission rates, and still other carriers may assume a better interest rate or mortality experience, among other pricing differential reasons. This is why it is important for the SPIA agent to know the carrier contract specifications and the market pricing drivers at any given point in time.

Illustration Elements

Name - this is usually the client/owner name but could also be the annuitant name if different from the SPIA proposed owner.

Agent's Name – agent contact information is listed in this section.

Illustration Date - is the date the illustration was produced by the agent or the home office and sets the annuity payment rate scale and the amount of time the illustrated rate scale is in effect. For example, the annuity rate scale might refer to a date several weeks previously and be good for all annuity quotes after that time.

Expiration Date - is the date the quote expires, usually ten days after the illustration date.

Deposit Date - is a term I dislike. I prefer "purchase date" because "deposit" implies something might be returned, such as a bank deposit or a brokerage deposit, and this may not be the case with a SPIA. This is the date on the illustration when the SPIA annuity premium is paid to the carrier.

Payment Date - refers to the initial payment date. For SPIAs on monthly payment mode, this date is usually thirty days after the deposit date, but this isn't required except with qualified SPIA contracts. Quarterly initial payments are usually deferred ninety days, while semiannual and annual payments are usually deferred 180 days to one year from their purchase dates respectively. For competing quote comparison purposes, it's important that each competitor's quote illustration use the same deferral times for their respective initial payments, as nonqualified SPIA contracts may start initial payments "off mode."

For example, one SPIA carrier may quote a monthly payment starting after thirty or sixty days, while another might quote a monthly payment starting immediately upon the SPIA contract issue date with no payment deferral. As long as the SPIA starts the initial payment within one year of the purchase date, the contracts receives all the associated tax benefits of a SPIA. But these off-modal initial payment quotes change the SPIA pricing and can cause consumers to make poor choices because the initial payment dates don't match from carrier to carrier. The agent should look for initial payment mismatches between competing quotes.

State - is important, as some states charge a SPIA premium tax determined by the state in which the owner resides. Annuity premiums are reduced by the state tax rate and forwarded to the state where the contract owner resides. The illustration "net premium," after the premium tax deduction (if any), needs to be used to calculate the illustrated SPIA payment. If the state listed on the illustration is incorrect, the illustration itself may be invalid.

Gender - refers to annuitant(s) gender, either male or female.

Age - is your age for the annuity pricing purposes. Depending on the carrier, this age may be your attained age or your nearest age give or take six months. Usually your date of birth is also displayed on the same line.

Cost Basis (nonqualified contracts only) - is the dollar amount of the premium that has already been taxed (income tax). For a cash premium payment, the cash payment amount is usually equal to the cost basis. If the SPIA annuity premium is being transferred from another deferred annuity or a life insurance policy, the cost basis will be what existed in the prior annuity or life insurance policy. The agent should inquire about obtaining the correct existing cost basis, as this will determine what, if anything will be the annual taxable income from the new SPIA contract.

For example, the cost basis (premium paid) transfer from the old deferred annuity or life insurance policy might be $50,000, but the cash transfer is $75,000 due to $25,000 of untaxed gains or the cash transfer might only be a $35,000 cash transfer due to $15,000 of losses. In many cases, cost basis utilization is a prime brokerage goal.

Nontaxable Amount (nonqualified contracts only) - is the amount of SPIA income that is not taxable and is determined in part by the cost basis and the IRS tables established for this particular SPIA.

Taxable Amount (nonqualified contracts only) - is the amount of SPIA income that is taxable and is determined by the SPIA earnings and the IRS table established for this particular SPIA. For qualified contracts like traditional IRAs, the entire SPIA income is taxable.

Payment Description - is the area on the illustration where the proposed SPIA is described. For example, it could say, ten-year period certain and have the potential for lifetime thereafter. There could also be a detailed payment description like the following:

This contract will provide periodic annuity benefit payments to the payee in the amount of $500.00, beginning 12/1/13. Periodic annuity benefit payments will continue monthly at the same amount for the period certain. At the end of the period certain:

a.) if the annuitant has died, the contract will terminate and periodic annuity benefit payments will cease; or

b.) if the annuitant has not died, the periodic annuity benefit payments will continue on the same basis as during the period certain. Upon death of the annuitant, the contract will terminate and the periodic annuity benefit payments will cease.

Form Number - is an important disclosure (see "Contract" chapter). This form number refers to the actual contract being illustrated and that you are purchasing in the state where you sign the application. If the form number that appears on the illustration doesn't match the form number on the actual SPIA contract you receive from the carrier, there is most likely a problem.

This Illustration Is Not A Contract - it's a disclosure. While a signed illustration (owner and agent both sign) accompanies the proposed SPIA application as part of the intention to purchase, it doesn't become part of the SPIA contract. By itself, the illustration doesn't bind the carrier to its quote.

Contract Combination Strategies

Purchasing SPIAs to provide for an element of a cohesive SPIA income plan is an art. Let's look at a few SPIA combination strategies that illustrate just how powerful and versatile these products are. All annuity rates are quoted at the time of writing.

Period Certain and Temporary Life

An eighty-year-old male with $250,000 is looking for a temporary income solution until the current interest rate levels climb to acceptable levels. At that time, he plans on redeploying assets to capture higher interest rates. He is willing to spend $50,000 now on an income annuity. If he doesn't survive the annuity duration, he wants his beneficiaries to receive at least some of the remaining payments following his death. He is willing to trade some of his legacy desires for a higher current income today.

Older annuitants receive higher annuity payments for life contingency annuity pricing versus period certain but only at the expense of legacy bequests. Period certain provides for superior legacy wishes, but because the current interest rate environment is poor, the period certain annuity payments are relatively small versus life contingent payments over the same duration and assuming equal premium costs.

In this case, trying to obtain the best of both worlds, an agent might suggest the use of a period-certain SPIA and a temporary-life SPIA combination. This strategy entails the use of two SPIAs issued from the same carrier or different carriers. Each contract produces initial monthly payments on the same payment date, and the contracts run concurrently. While the period-certain payment goes to the annuitant's beneficiary, the annuitant gets to collect a higher overall annual income with the integration of the temporary life contract.

In general, at current annuity rates, males of age seventy-five and females of age eighty or older receive increased payments for temporary life premiums versus period-certain premiums. The following charts (next page) shows the current pricing for an eighty-year-old male and two ninety-six-monthly payment (eight-year) duration contracts, one period certain and one temporary life.

Male, Age 80 (non-premium tax state)

Premium	Period Certain - Monthly	Temporary Life - Monthly
$50,000	$555.00	$670.00

The temporary life contract above produces about 20 percent more income per premium cost dollar versus the period-certain only contract. A simple division of the total $50,000 premium will produce a contract combination that provides higher income and legacy benefits versus the period-certain or temporary-life contracts separately.

For example, if the premium is divided equally between the two contracts, the combined monthly income is $613.00 with $278.00 being the legacy amount. If more income is wanted, then you simply allocate 75 percent—or $37,500—to the temporary-life contract with the balance of $12,500 to the period-certain contract. This produces a monthly income of $642.00, with $139.00 being the legacy benefit.

50% Allocation Each Contract

Annuity	Premium	Monthly Income
Period Certain (Legacy)	$25,000	$278.00
Temporary Life	$25,000	$335.00
Total	$50,000	$613.00

25% Allocation Period Certain & 75% Temporary Life

Annuity	Premium	Monthly Income
Period Certain (Legacy)	$12,500	$139.00
Temporary Life	$37,500	$503.00
Total	$50,000	$642.00

By allocating premium between these two contracts, individuals can simply dial in the amount of income versus legacy they desire. Since both contracts run concurrently over the eight-year duration, they both terminate when he turns eighty-eight.

Social Security Integrated Payments—Reducing SPIA Costs

One way of looking at overall "wealth" is the total "annuitized" wealth versus all other forms of wealth. Since annuitized wealth is attributable to SPIAs, defined benefit pension plans, and Social Security (SS) income, among other sources, it's all solely future income guarantees. Because of life-contingent payment pricing, usually there are no liquidity options with this kind of wealth. Younger individuals, ages fifty-five to sixty, might want to limit their income from annuitized wealth in order to free up assets for investment purposes.

Let's consider the following way to limit the cost of your total annuitized wealth by integrating it with future Social Security income.

A retired, sixty-year-old individual male needs $1,000 per month starting now and wants it to adjust 2 percent, compounded annually, for his lifetime. He is eligible to receive $750 per month with an annual COLA estimated at 2.00 percent from Social Security at age sixty-eight and does not want his "annuitized" wealth to exceed $1,000 per month, as he has legacy desires and wants to speculate with available assets in an attempt to increase his current wealth by investment returns.

To this end, he wants to control his SPIA costs today by integrating the SPIA income with his Social Security income starting at his age sixty-eight so that the combined total doesn't exceed $1,000 per month at that time. This can be achieved by a SPIA contract combination. The following charts highlight the SPIA cost for this monthly income with and without Social Security (SS) income integration.

Cash Refund Annuity 2.00% Annual Compounded COLA (without SS integration)

Annuity Premium	Initial Monthly Income	Refund Period Completes
$263,118	$1,000	18.50 Years

Let's look at a SPIA combination that will reduce his total SPIA costs today and provide him with the desired $1,000 monthly income of annuitized wealth integrated with his Social Security income starting eight years from now when he turns sixty-eight.

Annuity Contracts (with SS integration at age 68)

Annuity	Premium	Monthly Income Now (Age 60)	Annuity Income Age 68 (after 8-years w/2.00% COLA)
Cash Refund w2.00% COLA (Legacy)	$56,044	$213.00	$250.00
Period Certain (8-Years) Legacy	$75,552	$787.00	$0
SS Income at Age 68 (assumes a 2.00% COLA)	$0	$0	$750.00
Total	$131,596	$1,000.00	$1,000.00

By integrating his SS income starting in eight years with his annuity payments today, adjusted for the 2.00 percent annual COLA, he reduces his SPIA premium cost today from $263,118 to $131,596. This is a cost savings of $131,522.

The cash refund annuity premium payment of $56,044 funds a current monthly annuity payment of $213.00 that will grow to $250.00 after eight years. The period-certain annuity premium payment of $75,552 funds a current, monthly annuity payment of $787.00 for eight years that terminates at his age sixty-eight, leaving the $250.00 (adjusted) monthly cash refund annuity payment. When this annuity income is combined with his SS income at age sixty-eight (also adjusting for a 2.00 percent Annual COLA), his total monthly income remains at $1,000.00, and presto, you achieved your SPIA cost containment goal.

This individual could further lower his annuity premium purchase cost by an additional 7 to 8 percent if he used a combination of a life-only and temporary-life SPIA, but then there would be no annuity legacy benefit.

By using multiple SPIA contracts and integrating a future anticipated income—in this case the SS income—consumers can reduce their SPIA costs today. While SS income stops upon death, any annuity refund premium will be paid to his beneficiaries.

Income Tax Brokerage Strategies

Many SPIA brokerage strategies have their roots in income tax avoidance. Annuities remain, in general, tax-favored financial products. The key is utilizing all the available options.

Cost Basis Utilization Annuity and Life Insurance

Let's consider consumers who already own an existing deferred annuity or life insurance policy that contains a loss of premium. This is where the deferred annuity or life insurance policy has a current cash surrender value of less than the total premium cost. For example, individuals who purchased variable deferred annuities or some kinds of life insurance policies can experience losses versus the premiums they paid. In income tax lingo, the paid premium is referred to as the "cost basis."

Let's consider a consumer who paid $150,000 for a variable annuity several years ago at age sixty-five but now, at age seventy-five, needs income, but the contract cash value is only $93,000 due to losses over time. His tax bracket is 40 percent, and he can really use a tax advantage income source.

The goal is to utilize a period-certain annuity duration of just enough length to cover all his losses and create a source of nontaxable income. Nontaxable income is not the same as tax-free income that might be income taxable favorable in certain instances. Nontaxable income is never subject to income taxes. For example, tax-free income can be used to help determine taxation of Social Security income or the premium cost of your Medicare insurance coverage at age sixty-five.

In this case, at current annuity rates, a $93,000 annuity premium produces a period-certain only monthly income of $416.00 over thirty years or 360 months annuity duration. The total annuity payments are $149,760 ($416.00 x 360) which is less than his $150,000 cost basis; therefore, all this SPIA income is nontaxable! If there are any remaining payments at the annuitant's death, his beneficiaries also receive nontaxable income until all 360 monthly payments are made. In this case, the entire annuity gain of $56,769 ($149,769 - $93,000) was paid to the annuitant or the beneficiaries (depending on the case) without taxation of any kind.

Income Legacy Strategy
In addition to the above strategy incorporating an existing deferred annuity or life insurance policy containing a loss of premium, this strategy also passes a nontaxable income to beneficiaries when the annuitant dies, depending on the date of the annuitant's death.

Long Period Certain and Life
A wealthy individual's (father's) primary goal is to pass a tax-efficient income to his high-income beneficiaries—a fifty-five-year-old medical doctor son—as just one part of his estate. He is eighty years old and purchases a million-dollar, thirty-year period-certain and lifetime SPIA. This contract produces a monthly income of $4,553.00. Due to SPIA income tax treatment, the nontaxable portion is 61.70

percent or $2,809.00 with the remainder $1,744 taxable. Dad dies after five years at age eighty-five; the son is now fifty-five.

For this SPIA and upon Dad's death, the nontaxable portion changes to 100 percent because that's the tax benefit; the cost basis is paid first. After five years, Dad received $168,540 ($2,809 x 60 months) of his million-dollar tax basis. At this time, the remaining cost basis is $831,460 ($1,000,000 – $168,540). The remaining annuity at Dad's death is twenty-five period certain years (thirty total years – five paid years) or three hundred months.

Because the monthly payment is fixed at $4,553.00, the son receives this payment nontaxable for the next 182.61 months ($831,460 / $4,553.00) or 15.2 years (182.61 months / 12). The entire taxable portion to the son is deferred via an internal deferral established by the federal income tax policy until after 15.20 years or until the last 9.80 years when the entire annual income becomes taxable.

The son receives the nontaxable income during his high-wage years from ages fifty-five to sixty-five. The income from Dad's annuity will not be taxable to the son until he reaches age seventy (current age 55 + 15.20 years) when presumably he will be in a lower income tax bracket due to his own retirement. Of course, the longer Dad lives, the lower Son's inheritance. If Dad survives to age 110 and then dies, the annuity terminates without value.

Protection Strategy
A better way to provide a current income and an assured inheritance is through a joint and survivor option with an adult child. In this case, protection is paramount with tax benefits secondary.

Joint Annuitant Parents with Adult Kids (nonqualified)

In this case, an adult child who normally might be a beneficiary becomes an annuitant along with Dad. Both receive life contingent annuity payments. Dad receives these payments while he survives, and the adult child receives lifetime payments at Dad's death. All annuitants pay income tax according to the tax exclusion established on the annuity purchase date (unlike the long period certain and life explained in the previous example).

Since all the payments are life continent, they are, for all intents and purposes, only valuable to Dad and child. There is no probate, and the child just files a death claim, elects his own federal and state income tax withholding rate, and begins to receive payments.

You also see this strategy employed with grandchildren and spouses. The annuitant can rest assured it no longer matters how long he or she survives; if the child or joint insured survives them, then these individuals will inherit the payments—which is unlike period certain and life contracts that terminate after the period-certain period when the annuitant dies.

Because there are two joint-life contingent payments, the payment is lower than if there were just one life to consider. One way of increasing Dad's payment is to select a survivor income payment option of something less than 100 percent. If the payment reduces 50 percent on Dad's death to the surviving son, then Dad receives a higher income today. See below.

$50,000 Premium Dad Age 80, Son Age 55 (non-premium tax State)

Annuity Payment	Dad's Monthly Income	Son's Monthly Income
Life-Only on Dad	$441.00	$0
Joint 100% Survivor Son	$230.00	$230.00
Joint 50% Survivor Son	$300.00	$150.00

These are the kinds of payment reductions you see with parents and their adult children when dealing with qualified money (pretax) premiums like traditional IRAs.

Qualified Contract Strategies

Period Certain Features

While the impact of qualified money tax status on the premium funding affects SPIAs with period-certain, COLAs and joint and survivor options under the minimum distribution incidental benefit (MDIB) rules for required minimum distribution (RMD) purposes, as explained in the tax chapter, individuals can still incorporate beneficiary benefits. In some cases, the introduction of a reversionary annuity can circumvent some of the rules.

The key to maximizing SPIA beneficiary value is to know all the SPIA RMD rules. The other key is to understand not all carriers are willing to issue SPIA contracts that push the RMD limits.

For example, you are seventy-five years old and wish to purchase an IRA SPIA with the maximum period-certain benefit in favor of your beneficiary. Due to your age on December 31 of the year of purchase the IRS uniform lifetime table (ULT) states the maximum period-certain duration is 22.80 years or twenty-two years and nine months. This SPIA could also have a lifetime payment option. Some carriers may not want to issue SPIAs with period-certain durations that exceed twenty years. If you want to maximize your period-certain duration, you will have to hunt around for a carrier willing to issue to the maximum duration.

Let's say instead you are fifty years old and inherit a mutual fund IRA from your father. You make a timely election and become eligible to purchase a SPIA from an insurance company by transferring some or all of the inherited IRA to the insurance carrier. You have three main goals: provide for your own beneficiaries and potentially stretch out this inheritance to a subsequent generation; maintain the nonmarital property aspects of this property (because the SPIA is future income, it can't later become comingled with marital property), reduce your income tax bill by limiting your tax attributable to the SPIA annual income; and keep your inherited IRA out of your own possible future bankruptcy estate.

In the case of inherited IRAs, this fifty-year-old beneficiary cannot elect a period-certain duration that exceeds the duration outlined by the IRS single lifetime table (SLT) of 34.20 years or thirty-four years and three months. Again, if you want the maximum beneficiary benefit, you might have to hunt around to find a carrier who will issue this duration.

Cost of Living Adjustment (COLA) Features
To further enhance the beneficiary benefit on your own (un-inherited), IRA SPIA, you can incorporate either an annual or simple-compounded SPIA cost of living adjustment (COLA). To maximize this feature, the carrier performs a test by using the longer of the SLT or the period-certain duration, multiplies this period with the initial SPIA payment, and compares the product of these two numbers to the premium cost used to purchase the contract. The product has to be greater than the premium cost for the contract to qualify under the RMD rules. If the product is lower than the premium cost, the COLA is too high. High COLAs create large internal deferrals.

It may be carriers only wish to issue certain SPIA COLAs and then, only in whole percentages. The most common COLAs are 1.00 percent, 2.00 percent, and 3.00 percent compounded annually. Also, almost all field agent illustration software is limited to whole COLA elections, and the agent may not be aware fractional COLAs like 2.50 percent or 3.25 percent are available because they must be obtained via the home office quoting system.

To determine the maximum available COLA, the agent should make a special request to the carrier to determine what this COLA might be. Don't just accept what the field agent SPIA illustration system permits. An experienced SPIA agent will know of carriers that will issue fractional COLAs for SPIA RMD purposes.

Joint and Survivor Features
The IRS RMD rules primarily affect joint and survivor annuitants when spouses are not involved. In these cases, the joint annuitant is usually an adult child, a sibling, or a significant other. When the age difference between annuitants is more than ten years, there is an IRS table that limits the amount of the survivor benefit. The key thing is the table adjusts, depending on how old the IRA owner and joint annuitant were on the purchase date. The IRA owner always collects the entire payment even if his or her joint annuitant predeceases them.

Unlike the COLA test that has to been done by the carrier, a knowledgeable agent who knows the annuitants' dates of birth can just eyeball the IRS table to determine the maximum permitted survivor benefit.

The most common survivor payments offered by the average life insurance company are 100 percent, 66⅔ percent and 50 percent of the SPIA payment. If the SPIA payment is $1,000 and the survivor payment is 50 percent, the joint annuitant collects $500 upon the death of the IRA owner. However just like period-certain and COLA issues, you have to check with the carrier to see if it can maximize the IRS permitted survivor benefit.

Let's look at a case regarding significant others. An IRA owner who is seventy-two years old, purchases a joint and survivor annuity with his significant other, who is a fifty-nine-year-old male. They have been together for many years, and both have limited family support mechanisms, so they are more dependent upon each other.

The IRS table permits a 90 percent survivor benefit for this age combination. However, the agent and the consumer will have to make a home office inquiry to see if the carrier is willing to issue the maximum benefit.

Another case involves a forty-year-old terminally ill mother who wants to make sure her son, age ten, inherits what remains of her estate that's been ravaged by uninsured medical expenses. She has a lone remaining IRA, and while the additional SPIA income will be a blessing, her main concern is protecting her minor child via the life-contingent benefits of the contract. After her death, family members cannot be fully trusted to look out for the child's interests.

Normally in this case, because there is a thirty-year age difference, the maximum survivor benefit can't exceed 60 percent. However, because Mom is thirty years under age seventy (note being under age seventy at the SPIA purchase date is an exception), she can provide a 100-percent survivor benefit to her ten-year-old son.

This trick in this case is to find a carrier that is knowledgeable about this IRS SPIA rule and will issue such a contract with a ten-year-old annuitant. This is where working with a skilled agent can be as good as gold.

Incorporating Reversionary Annuities
One way of circumventing the joint and survivor IRS RMD rules for joint and survivor maximum benefits is to introduce a reversionary annuity (RA) if the IRA owner is insurable.

Qualified Premium Case
This case involves a sixty-five-year-old male and his significant other, a forty-five-year-old female. A SPIA is purchased to provide a survivor benefit for the female. They have been together for many years, and because of their age difference, the chances are very good the female will survive the male. The male is divorced from his first wife and can't depend on his adult kids to help take care of his significant other, so he established this IRA to help provide for her long-term financial interests. When he dies, his kids will be unable to interfere with her annuity payment. Since they are not married, the maximum benefit he can provide under the IRA rules is 84 percent. The most survivor benefit he can find available from any carrier is only 50 percent. The premium cost is $250,000. However, he really wants her to have a 100 percent survivor benefit. The following table displays the annuity choices available to him:

$250,000 Premium (non-premium tax state)

Annuity	Monthly Payment
Life-only (No legacy)	$1,403
JT & 50% Survivor Annuity	$1,131

Because he is insurable, the agent suggests he incorporate a reversionary annuity, which will provide a survivor annuity payment to the significant other of $1,403 per month upon his death. To fund the $450 monthly premium cost of the RA, the IRA owner elects the life-only annuity payment of $1,403 per month. This nets him a current income of $953.00 ($1,403 − $450) after the RA cost.

Because the IRA owner incorporated an RA, his beneficiary will receive the $1,402 under the tax rules for a SPIA (nonqualified). That means only about 20 percent or $280 of the monthly payment will be taxable. The remaining 80 percent is nontaxable until the annuity cost recovery is complete. This will be calculated by the RA carrier upon his death. If instead, he managed to provide her a survivor SPIA benefit monthly payment, 100 percent would be taxable as ordinary income under the IRA rules. So the RA gives her a much better after-tax income.

On the other hand, if she happens to predecease him and the RA terminates, he gets to stop paying the RA policy premium. This cost savings increase his income by $450 per month. RAs are covered more in depth in the "Worlds Collide" chapter.

Gifting Strategies

As reviewed at length in the tax chapter, a great annuity gifting strategy is to just convert nonmatured deferred annuities to matured contract(s). Then make gifts of the matured contracts to adult children.

A father has a $260,000 deferred annuity with a cost basis of $100,000. He has owned this contract for many years, but at age eighty-five realizes he will not need this asset and instead wants to gift it in equal shares to his four adult children with age ranges from sixty to sixty-five. However, he doesn't want to pay the income tax due on the $160,000 ($260,000 − $100,000) of contract gains. The agent suggests he conducts a 1035 exchange into four different SPIA contracts in equal shares. Each SPIA contracts receives $65,000 in premiums and has a cost basis of $25,000. He is now the owner or annuitant on each of the four SPIAs and each provides for period-certain payments over ten year durations.

At this point, he merely submits a change-of-ownership form with each of the four kids becoming the new owners and new beneficiaries of their respective SPIAs. The kids, as the new owners, pay all the income tax due on the SPIA payments at their income tax liability rates, and because they are also the new beneficiaries on their own contracts, they will inherit if Dad, who remains the annuitant, dies in the next ten years. The agent has to make sure the carrier will permit ownership changes on their SPIAs. Not all carriers permit contract ownership changes. This transaction doesn't address possible gift tax concerns.

Deferred Immediate Contracts
Deferred immediate contracts are also known as "deferred income annuity" (DIAs) have once again, in the past few years, become popular. DIA contracts are discussed in depth in the "Worlds Collide" chapter. Agents and consumers are still finding ingenious ways to incorporate this annuity design into the income planning landscape. Because these annuities are merely a guarantee of either period-certain or life contingent future income on one life or two lives, they have unique attributes for taxation and consumer protection. Some of these attributes are similar to those found in defined benefit pension plans offered by certain employers to their employees.

Business Ownership
DIAs opens up the prospect for business ownership. Normally, under the deferred annuity rules, corporate or other business entity owners don't qualify for the tax

deferral. However, because a DIA has no cash value or apparent interest accruals to tax from year to year, a business entity is not taxed on the deferred inside earnings of a DIA contract. So businesses could own such contracts for the benefit of their employees or corporate officers and receive the tax deferral. When the employees retire or otherwise leave employment, the contract titles could be transferred to them as the annuitant and they can receive the annuity payments as a form of deferred compensation and begin to pay income tax. Since this is not a "qualified" retirement plan, employers are free to establish their own parameters and agreements with each individual employee.

Split Case with SPIA and a DIA
One advantage of utilizing these two contracts in a combination transaction is to receive a more favorable internal tax deferral than available with just the SPIA alone. Individuals who are hyper sensitive to avoiding current income taxes because they are typically in higher income tax brackets might employ such a strategy.

For example, as a result of the recession, a fifty-five-year-old corporate officer has been pushed out of employment, and, as he can't retire just yet, he continues to do consulting work. While he is working part time, he is in the 50 percent income tax bracket. He considers purchasing a $500,000 SPIA ten-year period certain and lifetime thereafter (10CL) to help subsidize his annual wage income until he can fully retire at age sixty-five when he will be in a lower income tax bracket, estimated at 20 percent, and be more dependent on the SPIA income.

One choice is to purchase a single SPIA contract with this premium. In this case, his annual income is $27,636 and about 63 percent or $17,411 is excluded from income tax due to the IRS rules for annuities. As $10,225 is taxable, his after-tax income, being in the 50 percent income tax bracket, is $5,113, plus his excluded portion gives him a total after tax income of $22,524 (see table below).

Male Age 55 10CL

Premium	Annual Income	Excluded Portion 63%	Taxable Portion	After Tax Portion 50% Tax Bracket	Total After Tax Income
500,000	$27,636	$17,411	$10,225	$5,113	$22,524

Now let's look at alternate solution, a combination SPIA and DIA that offers a better internal deferral, reducing current income taxation. This keeps his tax liability low over the decades and actually costs him less initial premium.

The first contract is a SPIA for ten-year period certain only. The second contract is a DIA for a lifetime annuity with an initial ten-year deferral period. When you add the two contracts together, you still have a ten-year period certain with a lifetime payment thereafter. So, nothing has changed in this regard. When the ten-year period-certain SPIA contract completes its payments, then the DIA, with an initial ten-year deferral, begins its payments. The contract combination must also produce a consistent annual income of $27,636. The combined contracts premium cost should also be about $500,000. Let's look at the after tax benefits of this combination.

Male Age 55 Purchase Combination Split Case (10CL) Initial 10 Years

Contract	Premium	Annual Income	Excluded Portion 93%	Taxable Portion	After Tax Portion 50% Tax Bracket	Total After Tax Income
SPIA 10-Years Period Certain	$255,518	$27,636	$25,701	$1,935	$ 968	$26,669
DIA Deferred 10 years then Lifetime Only	$241,672	$0	$0	$0	$0	$0
Total	$497,190					

The object is to keep everything—the payment amounts, annuity terms, and premium costs—the same but change the amount of tax savings for the initial period, which is ten years in this case. This combo sale is actually cheaper—$497,190 vs. $500,000 for the SPIA. He gets a premium-cost savings of $2,810 right out of the gate.

Male Age 55 Purchase Combination Split Case (10CL) After 10 Years

Contract	Premium	Annual Income	Excluded Portion 43%	Taxable Portion	After Tax Portion 20% Tax Bracket	Total After Tax Income
SPIA 10-Years Period Certain	$255,518	$0	$0	$0	$0	$0
DIA Deferred 10 years then Lifetime Only	$241,672	$27,636	$11,883	$15,752	$12,602	$24,485
Total	$497,190					

In both cases, the SPIA and the split case, his annual income is the same at $27,636 per year. However because of the split case, he enjoys significant after-tax income of $26,669 versus the SPIA case alone, which would be $22,542.

This increase of $4,127 per year allows him to put $41,270 of additional after-tax income into his pocket. The terms of the split-case annuity are the same: ten years guaranteed, then lifetime income thereafter. In addition, this split case also offers him a premium-cost savings of $2,810 out of the gate. A possible premium-cost savings is also a very good reason to look at split cases, because the cost saving can be a nice additional benefit.

Assuming he survives the initial ten years, let's look at what happens after this time. While his income stays the same at $27,636, the total after-tax amount, while higher in the first ten years at $26,669 versus $22,524 for the SPIA, decreases to $24,485 versus the SPIA amount of $25,591 (now 20% tax bracket). The DIA contract had ten deferral years prior to making the first income payment, so the taxable portion is higher, but because his income tax bracket is also reduced due to full retirement, his total after-tax income is only slightly lower than the SPIA by itself. In the meantime, he enjoyed over $40,000 of additional total after-tax income during the initial ten contract years.

The split case also provides an agent the opportunity to find the best pricing for each component—the ten-year period-certain SPIA for the initial ten years and then the ten-year DIA contract for the lifetime component for the subsequent period following the initial ten years.

Impaired Annuitant Risk
In all the cases we referenced so far, the SPIA pricing assumption is all the annuitants will live normal life

expectancies for any given individual's age and gender. This is sometimes referred to as a standard life expectancy. However, this may not always be the case. There are a few SPIA carriers who will consider ill health due to sickness or injury of the insured or annuitant when determining how much annual income they will pay versus any premium cost or, conversely, how much premium-cost savings they will offer for any given annual income. This is often referred to as "impaired risk" underwriting.

More commonly found in the structured settlement annuity industry, this technique is available to consumers and can benefit those annuitants who really need the SPIA income from a safety perspective because they can't replace lost money like a healthy person might be able to do. In other words, their income is everything because their ability to work and earn a wage is significantly reduced due to their health or injury circumstances.

Typically, the unhealthy person's lifetime expectations need to be substantially impacted for them to receive a pricing concession from the annuity company—but not so impacted they might die in a few years. For this technique to apply, the SPIA must contain some life-contingent payments. SPIAs that are exclusively period-certain payments cannot benefit from this technique.

The insurance company underwriter, the person who reviews medical records the annuitant provides, determines the annuitant's adjusted life expectancy due to his or her health circumstances. The agent prepares the annuity application with the medical records or might just submit medical records prior to taking an application to determine what the underwriter will consider.

After a favorable medical record review, the underwriter assigns a "rated age" to the annuitant, and while the annuitant may be age sixty-eight chronologically, his or her rated age might be seventy-five. A sixty-eight-year-old female can purchase an installment refund SPIA for $150,000 and receive a monthly income of $784 with $588 excluded from taxation. However, with a rated age of seventy-five, the monthly income increases to about $917. This is a about a 17 percent increase in monthly income. The nontaxable amount established by IRS tables remains the same at $588.

At age seventy-five, she has a shorter life expectancy than she does at age sixty-eight. Because the underwriter believes even though she is sixty-eight years old chronologically, she actually has the normal life expectancy of a female at age seventy-five.

Some of the illnesses that will qualify for medically impaired risk consideration are heart attacks, cancer, diabetes, Parkinson's, ALS, MS, renal failure, and Alzheimer's. Some of the injuries that will qualify are paraplegia or quadriplegia, traumatic brain injury (TBI), mental retardation, and significant burns causing lung damage.

Chapter Summary
• During the annuity brokerage process, the annuity illustration the agent provides is crucial for determining current annuity pricing and tax benefits. The correct data is needed for accuracy and ease of comparison with annuity pricing from other insurance companies.

• To achieve your desired results, you may have to combine SPIA contracts strategically. Since SPIA payments may have different attributes, you can combine the payment variety to create a custom SPIA arrangement to meet almost any need.

• Fully utilizing annuity or life insurance cost basis is an important SPIA brokerage goal. This can be accomplished with a full or partial 1035 exchange from a deferred annuity contract or a life insurance policy to a SPIA contract. It can also be accomplished by exercising the annuity options in the existing deferred annuity or life insurance policy. These options may be exercised by owners or beneficiaries.

• Qualified SPIAs must conform to the IRS's required minimum distribution (RMD) rules for IRAs and qualified retirement plans as modified by the IRS minimum distribution incidental benefit (MDIB) rules.

• After annuity company review, annuitants with impaired health and/or significant injuries may qualify for improved annuity pricing when they select life-contingent annuity payments.

PROTECTION

"Be sure you put your feet in the
right place, then stand firm."
—*Abraham Lincoln, sixteenth president*

Introduction

Safety is the number-one reason why individuals should purchase these contracts. The safety element of a SPIA is both sublime and subtle. The sublime speaks to its design, which is different from any other financial product and can be a double-edged sword. As one of the most powerful financial mechanisms an individual can purchase, the design alone protects individuals to the highest degree possible.

Some might argue a portfolio of US Treasury Securities holds the top dog spot when it comes to safety. But these in-the-know financial types say this because they are solely addressing default risk. The risk the federal government will not honor its debt and default to bond holders is considered nonexistent. However, as we all know, default risk is merely a single risk. There are all kinds of other risks consumers face in everyday life that a simple US Treasury Securities portfolio does not address. As far as default risk goes, we will see how SPIAs are backed by insurance carriers and the legal reserve system and other protections. Putting them at least on par with the federal government while simultaneously addressing the everyday consumer risks is where the SPIA really shines. This is what tips the scale in favor of the SPIA, making them the superior protection product choice.

One huge and always-imminent risk SPIAs address every day is dissipation risk. Dissipation risk is basically all the ways individuals can lose assets after they have been acquired and accumulated, and there are a lot of them. As we will see, SPIAs are primarily defensive financial products. Some of these risks are ugly and don't make pleasant dinner conversations, and they are certainly not sexy. They are just devastating. It's up to the agent to raise questions about potential dissipation risks to determine just what these might be when presenting a SPIA purchase to a suitable client.

Dissipation Risks

At the onset, one characteristic of a dissipation risk is the usually lightning-quick nature of the strike. It's the kind of thing you usually hear other people speak of with comments like, "I can't believe my life has changed so dramatically" or "I never thought something like this would ever happen to me" or "Yesterday, things were so different than they are today." If we haven't heard these comments personally or on television, certainly we have all read them somewhere— perhaps in the local paper or in a magazine.

Many people live on a financial trapeze without too much net beneath them. Any event, such as a loss of a business or even a rapid succession of multiple events like a loss of a business and a divorce, may send the average person into a financial tailspin. Or perhaps even a major casualty that leads to a loss of a business and a divorce for a triple whammy.

Other individuals experience major physical and cognitive heath declines that can lead to devastating financial impacts. Physical injuries can lead to salary interruptions that affect your abilities to accumulate wealth and also to retain the wealth you already have. Cognitive health declines can affect your abilities to control your wealth, causing you to rely on others who may not have your best interests at heart.

Then there are individuals who become overwhelmed by debt who, after exhausting resources, turn to various lenders in a final attempt at a financial rescue that, more often than not, results in bankruptcy, forcing them into the ranks of the dispossessed.

Many become embroiled in legal affairs steaming from the above situations, but there are also others, like civil-asset forfeitures. These individuals not only face adverse settlements and judgments, but also soaring legal representation costs that hammer future financial prospects.

I'm not in the financial planner camp that believes one has a duty to society to become completely indigent and say, "We faced adversity and we tried and failed; now we can fall on our swords." I believe individuals with even modest means, if at all possible, have a duty not to become indigent in the first place and fall back on the good graces of society and or their extended families or their children.

SPIAs help prevent poverty, and ultimately, if you ever get into a real financial jam and all your investments (stock, bonds, mutual funds), cash-value life insurance policies, deferred-annuity contracts, and real estate are gone, SPIAs will invariable become your last-surviving asset, the last man standing, and the thing that permits you some small measure of financial dignity (see "Anecdote" chapter). Unless God spied you from above, parted the clouds, put his hand on your should, and said, "I like you; you're special, and I'm not going to let anything happen to you...," you are completely underestimating your prospects of financially fairing from a well-timed financial shock or shocks.

While SPIAs stop the financial bleeding because of the insurance mechanisms they are, like all matters of insurance, you need to own the contracts before you need them in order to obtain the desired benefits. This is certainly true for older individuals who purchase traditional SPIAs and also true for younger individuals who are now able to purchase deferred-income annuity (DIA) contracts (see chapter "When Worlds Collide").

Contract Design

From a design prospective, what make SPIA contracts so special? The design is a critical element to the protection against dissipation risks. A SPIA is irrevocable, and its payments are not commutable back to lump sums. Also, SPIAs that pay life-contingent payments are really of value to no one other than their contract owners whose lives they are paid on. This commitment to future income is what makes it possible not to go broke in the present. There is no immediate cash value, but rather a future income that is only paid if you live. People who own life-contingent SPIA contracts are well-protected against other people. Anything that erodes this simple formula also erodes your ultimate protection of future income.

With the possible exception of an owner change (if the SPIA even permits this) there are only a few other changes permitted. The key person or persons, the annuitant(s), and the measuring life or lives for the payments may never be changed. Beneficiaries or payees may be changed by the owner or someone legally acting on the owner's behalf, such as a conservator or even a power of attorney (POA), but if an irrevocable beneficiary exists, then the owner or legal representatives of the owner cannot make this change unilaterally but must first seek the written permission of the irrevocable beneficiary.

SPIA owners might convert the annuity payment's physical check into an electronic funds transfer (EFT) or perhaps changing banking instructions. Certainly the annuity income, after it is paid, may end up dissipated or otherwise temporarily manipulated, but the annuity contract for the future income cannot become so manipulated.

For example, the most assured way an individual can pass a legacy to a particular child is to make the child part of the contract as a joint annuitant. This is one way of providing a legacy benefit that is also life contingent while protecting both the father or mother and the child. The parent receives an irrevocable income only paid if they live, which isn't valuable to others, and at the parents' death, the child receives the income that is only valuable to the child and can't, for example, ever fall into the child's martial estate (see chapter on "Marital Property").

The parent in the above example or even a much-younger business owner with a deferred income annuity (DIA) contract who is suffering from a business failure can't go back to the insurance company or even be compelled by a third party to request a lump sum amount from SPIAs or DIAs that have been in force for many years. The key is the words "in force for many years" are a requirement.

Remember, just like in all matters of insurance, you need to own a SPIA or DIA before you can call on all its benefits. Generally, you cannot enter into legal contracts for the sole purposes of diminishing the value of your assets or making your assets unavailable to your creditors or others who may have a legal interest in them. This is referred to as "fraudulent transfer" and is not a legal activity. Such transfers are now governed by the new Uniform Voidable Transaction Act of 2014 (UVTA) adopted by the Uniform Law Commission on July 16, 2014. Any nearing or potentially crossing the line here should be thoroughly discussed with competent legal counsel.

Rating Agencies

There are several companies that make it their business to evaluate and rate life insurance companies based on their financial strength. These companies are the A.M. Best Company; Standard & Poor's; Moody's Investors Service; Weiss Research; and Fitch Ratings, Inc. While their methodologies differ, these firms typically assign letter ratings to companies' financial strength starting from the strongest, A (or some variation), and going down through F (and associated variations). Consumers may want to consider only those companies rated A (or some variation of A) unless there are extenuating circumstances, such as exceptional pricing or unique contract features.

Legal Reserve System

The legal reserve system is a state imposed financial system that keeps insurance companies solvent. This is why life insurance companies are usually referred to as legal reserve life insurance companies. Since this system is established by a body of state laws, it is also referred to as a "statutory" system.

This means insurance companies report all matters to the state. The state monitors insurance carrier financial activities via a series of audits and report reviews. In fact, all aspects of the insurance carriers' activities are reviewed by the state. This includes their investments, financial reserves, capital investments, financial statements, business activities and product approvals (see "Contract" chapter), which all have to fit within state guidelines.

The legal reserve system requires carriers post reserves (real money) to back their contractual guarantees. The state makes sure, in their opinion, the insurance company has real money or other assets in place in sufficient quantities to protect all contract holders.

Reinsurance
This is an insurance carrier technique of transferring risks to other insurance companies or entities that absorb all or part of some identified risk. It's a technique that permits carriers to manage their profits and capital requirements or needs. While there are different kinds or reinsurance agreements, and the transactions can be fairly complex, the good news is states also review these transactions.

State Resources
Since states predominantly regulate and control insurance company activities, consumers need to contact their respective state insurance departments regarding what state safeguards, if any, extend to their particular annuity contracts or other insurance policies. By state law, it is illegal for agents to disseminate the details of state resource information.

A centralized source of state information is maintained by the National Organization of Life and Health Insurance Guaranty Associations (NOLHGA). NOLHGA a voluntary association was formed in 1983 and its mission is to coordinate state efforts to protect consumers living in different states. NOLHGA can be found at http://www.nolhga.com/.

State Court Legal Protections
Another protection afforded to annuity contracts and not to other financial products with the exception of life insurance, is one by our state court systems. Over the years, state courts have recognized the benefits of annuity contracts to society because they help prevent poverty by ultimately helping to keep people off the public dole.

This just reinforces my contentions made throughout this book annuity contracts are more about defensive financial posturing than getting rich. In other words, you don't purchase annuities to get rich; you buy them to keep from going broke.

Bankruptcy
Bankruptcy usually occurs when a debtor declares it in order to obtain relief from their creditors. Individuals usually file for such protection under chapter 7 of the law in United States bankruptcy courts. Individual debt maybe discharged (forgiven), restructured, or a combination of both. There is also involuntary bankruptcy. This is when a creditor or a group of creditors can compel your bankruptcy (which is outside the scope of this discussion).

While bankruptcy cases are filed in United States bankruptcy court as part of the United States district court system for claim validity and exemptions, they are often dependent on state law. State law plays a major role in consumer bankruptcy cases. Because there are fifty states, bankruptcy laws are not entirely uniform, as each state exercises its own rules.

In various degrees, annuities enjoy exempt property status for personal bankruptcy actions in just about every state. Exempt property means the property is not included in your bankruptcy estate when the court sums all your assets and liabilities (debts owed). Some states have exemption limits. They feel annuity proceeds or value necessary to "reasonably" support the contract owner and their dependents are permissible. Then there are other states like Colorado, Florida, Illinois, Michigan, and Texas that permit unlimited protections of amounts used to purchase annuities regardless of having dependents as beneficiaries. There are some states that offer no annuity protection, such as Connecticut, Massachusetts, Montana, New Hampshire, and Virginia, to name a few.

However, contracts typically have to be purchased in exempt states, by residents of these states, who may have been required to establish residency over a period of time, such as six months or even a year. In other words, you can't purchase an annuity in New York, then move to Florida and enjoy Florida state annuity protections.

A seventy-five-year-old consumer who owns a life contingent annuity that was purchased several years ago, who is currently receiving $1,000 per month, and who also has a single creditor seeking judgment to satisfy a $50,000 debt, might be able to retain the entire annuity payment if that payment is keeping him or her off the street.

On the other hand, if the monthly annuity payment was $5,000, the debt was $1 million, the annuity owner had other assets that totaled $500,000, and there were several debtors, the debtors may enter into an agreement to take the other assets in satisfaction of the entire debt rather than trying to collect some portion of their debt from the annuity contract. After all, if the creditor elects to take some portion of the monthly payment in lieu of some of the other assets, which the court deems over and above the amount reasonably and necessary to support the owner and his or her dependents (whatever that amount is), succeeds in this effort, and then the owner dies, so does the creditors' monthly collection of the payment. They may just forgo any interest in the annuity contract because they're not willing to risk their debt judgment and collection on the owner's life contingency and just settle on the other assets that are more readily available.

This makes sense for a SPIA, but what about a DIA? DIA contracts will be discussed at length in the chapter "When Worlds Collide." Since a DIA design is relatively new on the annuity scene, they will need to be evaluated by the bankruptcy courts on a case-by-case basis as the need arises.

But let's look at the dilemma. Now, you have a forty-five-year-old person purchasing a fixed and irrevocable DIA that doesn't commence life contingent payments for twenty years at his or her age sixty-five. At that time, the monthly income is $1,000, paid for his or her lifetime. If he or she files for chapter 7 bankruptcy at age fifty-five, there are still ten deferral years before the first monthly payment even starts. From a creditor's point of view, the DIA is even more unattractive than the SPIA. The owner's death terminates the contract.

But not all annuity contracts are 100 percent single- or joint-life contingent. Some, as we have seen, include period-certain payments or are entirely period-certain payments. In these cases, it may be possible for a third party (see "Third Party" chapter) to purchase some or all of the period-certain payments and provide some cash that a bankruptcy judge may order.

A case I followed for several months occurred in Montana. Now, Montana offers no protections to annuity holders in bankruptcy court. However, the SPIA design appeared to protect the owner quite nicely. The annuity was purchased many years prior to the owner's bankruptcy, and the judge in this case ordered the payments put out to the highest bidder. The annuity had ninety remaining guaranteed payments with the rest of the payments life contingent, paid on the joint life of the annuitant and his "significant other."

To the judge's dismay, while he was able to secure a few bidders for the ninety remaining guaranteed payments, no third party bidders emerged to take the life-contingent payments. The annuitant was an older man, and by operation of the contract, upon his death it passed to his significant other, who was not a party to the bankruptcy. Also, the judge was unable to order health records regarding the annuitant because they were protected by the Health Insurance Portability and Accountability Act of 1996 ("HIPAA"), federal privacy laws. Given the fact the annuitant was an older male, whose health could not be ascertained for the purpose of his bankruptcy and annuity transaction, no bidders emerged for the life-contingent annuity element of the contract and it remained intact. I don't know about the other bankruptcy estate assets but, I suppose in this case, the creditors had to satisfy themselves with these.

This is prime example of how annuities keep you from going broke and protect your loved ones. If this annuity had, for example, been a deferred cash-value annuity, mutual fund, bank certificate of deposit, or even a US treasury bond portfolio, the entire asset possibly would have ended up in the hands of his creditors.

Bankruptcy of Your Beneficiaries
It's just not your bankruptcy! SPIAs also work to protect your beneficiaries from their own financial disasters. The State in which your beneficiary resides will control the bankruptcy

rules. Beneficiaries who inherit SPIA payments from IRA or other nonqualified contracts as joint annuitants, technically per the annuity contract, are not beneficiaries because they are joint insured (annuitants). The payments are made on their lives with no opportunities for withdrawing funds, other than the monthly payment, from the contract.

Medicaid
Medicaid is a federal program, administered by the states, which provides health coverage for some low-income people, families, children, pregnant women, elderly, and people with disabilities. Medicaid programs must follow federal guidelines, but they vary somewhat from state to state. Under Medicaid, individuals can be covered for long-term care (LTC) services if they meet several general and financial requirements. There is a history regarding SPIA annuity contracts and Medicaid planning. How the states look at SPIA ownership for Medicaid eligibility purposes has changed over the years.

The Deficit Reduction of 2005 was signed into law on February 8, 2008, and affected the use of SPIAs for Medicaid planning purposes.

Once you become medically eligible, there are also financial requirements in order to collect benefits. There are income tests and asset tests to help determine financial need and eligibility. These tests are conducted in the light of a five-year history preceding an application for Medicaid benefits.

SPIA contracts purchased outside this five- year period are generally ignored for the asset test, but annuity income will be counted for the income test. But depending on the contract and the length of benefit claim, much of the beneficiary income may pass to contract beneficiaries, and certainly all income passes to joint annuitants (spouses and children), insured individuals who are not technically beneficiaries according to the annuity contract.

Annuity contracts purchased within the five-year period prior to making a claim for Medicaid benefits for long-term care are closely scrutinized and, depending on the state, must meet certain requirements or financial consequences may be imposed. This is outside the scope of the book, and I strongly urge individuals to work closely with an elder law attorney or estate planning attorney when purchasing SPIA contracts and also simultaneously contemplating Medicaid benefit eligibility.

SPIAs that are also IRAs or ROTH IRAs may be extended additional protections regardless of purchase dates. So, work with an elder law attorney when dealing with these qualified contracts.

The key with SPIAs and Medicaid as with all things insurance is to buy the SPIA years before you need the benefits.

Reversionary Annuities (RA) Unique Protection Roles
It appears one of the best protection financial products is the reversionary annuity. While its structure will be fully covered in the chapter called "When Worlds Collide," the ownership of such a product protects owners from quite the laundry list of bad stuff.

While an RA is a life insurance policy, unlike other life insurance products, it provides the policy beneficiary with a lifetime annuity income when the insured dies. The RA has no cash value, unlike universal life or whole life insurance. In lieu of cash value, this survivor annuity payment vests over the premium payment duration. If the beneficiary or survivor benefit is $1,000 per month upon my death, I might become 50 percent vested after five years or twenty years depending on the premium payment terms of the policy I elected. So, should I lapse the policy for nonpayment of premium for whatever reason, I can't lose my vested survivor benefit.

Typically, if you have a universal life or whole life insurance policy and you don't pay the annual premiums, you run a high probability of lapsing the policy and having nothing to show for it.

The noncash value aspect of the policy keeps it out of the Medicaid estate. So, consumers will be able to maintain their RAs and qualify for Medicaid assuming all the other Medicaid-qualifying steps are taken. If they become too sick or infirmed and can no longer afford to make the premium payment, the RA survivor annuity benefit vesting schedule will insure some portion of the annuity income makes it to your beneficiary.

In the marital property chapter, spousal beneficiaries must account for the deferred income value of the RA policy and shift other marital property to the owner or insured spouse (see the "Marital Property" chapter). In this manner, the owner or insured spouse receives funds in order to help pay premiums of the beneficiary spouse's lifetime annuity benefit.

In a bankruptcy, there isn't any cash value, and the policy falls outside the bankruptcy estate. So, if you own such a policy and suffer a business failure or other financial loss, you will be able to retain your policy.

Chapter Summary
• Safety is the main reason for purchasing SPIAs because they provide antidissipation benefits: unlike other financial

products, their illiquid design and life-contingent payment design make them very unattractive to third parties.

• The legal reserve system, reinsurance, state resources, and state court legal protections also work to protect SPIA contract owners and their beneficiaries. SPIA contract owners (and possibly contract beneficiaries) enjoy some protections that exclude SPIAs, up to certain limits and under certain conditions, from the bankruptcy and Medicaid estates.

• Reversionary annuities have unique protection roles: the insured and the beneficiary are established on the purchase date and can't be changed. Depending on the premium payment history, the policy either can't lapse or can only partially lapse after a number of premium payment years. There are no policy cash values for the owner or the beneficiary who receives a lifetime-only payment when the insured dies. Because there are no policy cash values, RAs receive exemptions from both bankruptcy and Medicaid estates.

MARITAL PROPERTY ASPECTS OF SPIAS/DIAS/RAS

"Getting to the top is optional;
getting down is mandatory."
—*Ed Viesturs, high altitude mountaineer*

"Hell is empty and all the devils are here."
—*William Shakespeare*

Introduction

I think one of the biggest deficits with your average financial planner is what I call the implicit sunny-day assumption that's used when they plan portfolios and consumption pro-files. They often fail to consider dissipation risks that may affect client assets. In most of the cases, their risk definition primarily involves the "investment" risk and some standard withdrawal rate risk. In reality, this is just too narrow. While they may make allowances for other insurance matters like life, health, disability, property, and casualty, they forget about or don't consider the income-producing assets. After all, income producing assets are the mother's milk for all retirees and also non-retirees.

Many financial planners just automatically assume investments are made, returns are realized, and reasonable withdrawals or consumption emerges and then consumers just wander off into the sunset, happily ever after. Any consumer living any kind of unsheltered life knows in his or her heart this scenario is probably not likely to occur without experiencing some bumps in the road.

One of several financial bumps in the road can be divorce. While my experience gives me a unique point of view in this regard versus other financial planners', the aspect of divorce in our society is prevalent and its financial effects so potentially devastating an entire chapter of this book is dedicated to it. Once again, I will illustrate the magnificent owner protection aspects of DIA and SPIA contracts versus any other asset.

As the incidents of SPIA and now newer deferred income annuity DIA design contracts issuance continue to rise, so does the probability these contracts will begin appearing in marital estates. For many couples without agreements to the contrary, a marital estate is created for all property acquired by either spouse after the marriage date, regardless of which spouse actually holds title to the property.

SPIAs with payments starting within twelve months of the purchase date are prominently purchased by older individuals, specifically those ages sixty-five and up, and presumably in longer-term marriages—those that aren't too affected by the specter of divorce. However, Pandora 's Box was open in the marital property world with the advent and reintroduction of deferred income annuities (see "When Worlds Collide" chapter), often purchased by much younger individuals. With more than $2 billon sold each year, DIA contracts are now becoming a force on the national screen. The more DIAs are purchased by younger individuals, the more likely these properties are to appear in marital estates.

As the national economy continues to degrade and make tectonic economic shifts, marriages, particularly younger marriages of less than ten years, will increasingly become subject to rising economic pressures. Many experts expect this rising economic pressure to contribute to the national marriage failure rate.

The Uniform Marital Property Act (UMPA) promulgated by the Uniform Law Commissioners in 1983 provides the basis for what is and is not marital property.

So, what makes SPIAs and DIAs so difficult to evaluate and to divide the marital interest as opposed to other financial assets? In a nutshell, it's illiquidity. Illiquidity is both the bane and the benefit of these contracts. Much of the bane or benefit allocation depends on which spouse you are relative to the parties on the contract in question. SPIAs and DIAs can't become separated into pieces; typically there are no cash-surrender values or payment-commutation privileges and COLAs, period-certain durations, and rights of survivorship can't be altered after the contract issue date.

SPIA/DIA Marital Interest—Single Life
The timing of cash contributions, which, in this case, is paid premiums, determines marital interest. If contributions are made during the marital period, they are marital property and the earnings are marital property. If contributions are made prior to the date of marriage or after the marital interest ends, then these are separate property contributions. State laws determine when the marital interest ends. In some states, the ending period is the date of physical separation, while in others it is the date the marital dissolution legal action commences. You will have to check the state law in your individual state for more information.

Of course, just as in other matters there are some exceptions. One exception is whether the contributing spouse can prove his or her contributions made during the marital period were derived from a separate property source. This source could be funds accumulated prior to the marriage and not commingled with other marital funds. The funds could also be derived from noncommingled funds specifically derived from exempt sources like inheritance, disability, Social Security benefits, or funds from the settlement of a personal injury. The burden of proof regarding any separate property claim rests solely on the spouse making the claim.

One advantage of a single premium SPIA or DIA is the ease of marital property interest determination. If the contract was purchased prior to any marriages, then it will never become marital property. Accretions of value over time attributable to a single premium source retain the same interest, marital or nonmarital, relative to the funding source. SPIA and DIA contracts are matured and vested on their purchase dates because annuity payment pricing is set immediately and guaranteed by its respective contract at the time of premium payment.

However, some DIA contracts are flexible premium payment design contracts. This means you can make monthly or annual premium payments to a single contract and the sum of all the payment purchases are added together to determine your total annuity income at the payment commencement date. These contract designs may contribute to a mixed property. If it is determined 70 percent of the funds were marital contribution, then 70 percent of the property is marital and 30 percent of the property is nonmarital or separate property. This will end up being an important determination when and if the contract benefits become divided. A major problem in the determination of marital property interest in any financial asset is a melding of both separate and marital property interest in the same financial product. Invariably, some portion will be marital as opposed to exclusively separate property.

This is the same problem people have with IRAs and other contributory retirement plans like 401(k)s and defined benefit pensions. Contributory retirement plans receive contributions over many years and defined benefit plans accrue value based on the passing of working years and the plan formula.

For example, I'm forty and purchase a life-only IRA DIA contract with a payment commencement date at my age sixty-five and begin to make annual IRA contributions for three years that ultimately produce a total monthly income of $500. At age forty-three, I marry and continue to make annual IRA contributions that produce a total $1,000 in monthly income, and then divorce after ten years at age fifty-three. I continue to make payments for seven more years, which totals another $750 in monthly income.

The total monthly income at age sixty-five is $2,250 ($500 + $1,000 + $750), but of this amount, $1,000 is marital property. If the marital portion is divided equally, I would receive $500 plus all my separate property income of $1,250 ($500 + $750) for a total of $1,750.

Valuation

I often hear the question: If you are just going to divide the payment, then why is valuation of the payment important? First of all, the payment may not even be subject to division primarily because the nonannuitant spouse really doesn't want anything to do with it. If you take the above example, why would the nonannuitant spouse be interested? If I'm the annuitant, the annuitant can't be changed by operation of the contract; the contract has no cash surrender value and terminates upon my death. If the payment is divided in the above IRA example and I die, my spouse's payment portion also terminates.

As the nonannuitant spouse, the thought of sharing a payment and entwining my fate with my soon-to-be ex-spouse for the rest of my post-divorce life is completely unpalatable when what I really want is to foster a "clean break" from him or her.

For all practical purposes, such a contract is completely unattractive to the nonannuitant spouse, and this is exactly why the parties to the contract matter. This speaks directly to the defensive nature of the financial product. Owners or annuitants are better protected from third-party interests even if those interests are your spouse's or soon to be ex-spouse's. This product design persuades the nonannuitant spouse to forgo his or her marital interest in exchange for something more immediate and tangible with equal or at least "perceived" equal value.

So, what is the value of such an interest? One acceptable valuation method a court or a judge will consider is the "replacement cost" method. The replacement cost for the above annuity is just the current cost to purchase a duplicate contract. In this case, the cost can be determined by just asking the insurance company for a quote for the current premium cost for the marital share.

For example, at the time of divorce, for a fifty-three-year-old male annuitant, the premium cost for $1,000 monthly annuity starting in twelve years at age sixty-five for a life-only IRA annuity is about $95,000. This is the de facto value of the marital portion.

If the above marital value were to be divided evenly $47,500 ($95,000 x 50 percent) would get credited to her, the nonannuitant spouse. If another liquid IRA doesn't exist from which he can withdraw this payment then the payment may have to come from a post-tax source; this creates an income tax consideration as well because the IRA is pretax money.

In this case, he keeps the entire IRA DIA contract in exchange for an IRA cash payment of $47,500 to her from another liquid IRA. Of course, for various reasons there could be an unequal division but this topic is outside this book's scope.

The marital estate may also contain multiple retirement plans. For cost control purposes, it would be more cost effective to value the marital interest in each plan, trade the values off, and then physically divide the remaining plan to net the difference out in order to equalize the total retirement benefits versus the legal costs to divide each retirement plan's marital interest.

However, is the above really a "fair exchange" just by looking at the nominal dollars? Not really. The annuity is guaranteed by a legal reserve life insurance company. It can't become dissipated over the life of the contract. These are two unique coexisting benefits not present in any other financial arrangement.

The odds are very much against this nonannuitant spouse taking the $47,500 cash payment, investing it over a ten- to fifteen-year deferral period (assuming she is age fifty) and then continuing to invest it over the rest of her life expectancy in such a manner as to support a $500-monthly income. There are just too many unknowns besides the financial markets that might affect her over such a long duration of time.

People remarry and have opportunities to comingle property; they become ill or injured and suffer career interruptions; they lose businesses, get sued and have to hire attorneys and possibly pay for settlements or judgments; they can suffer casualty losses and so on. A lot could possible happen over long durations of time. It's not just the specter of financial market loss that dissipates assets.

In a perfect world, a truly fair division utilizing the $47,500 IRA cash transfer would call for the nonannuitant spouse to purchase her own monthly payment DIA starting at her desired date and paid over her life expectancy. This might not generate the same monthly income due to gender and the payment start date selection, but, it would be the "actuarial equivalent" or equal to her share of his $500-monthly benefit starting at his age sixty-five.

Unfortunately, DIA and SPIA contracts do not have contractual provisions for cancelling contracts and reissuing new ones to accommodate property separation needs when a couple divorces. To do so, his contract would suffer a benefit reduction and a new contract would have to be issued to her for her $47,500 premium share. Additionally, the carrier is at risk due to "anti-selection" (see "Pricing" chapter). The now (at the time of divorce) severely ill or injured annuitant spouse would have the opportunity to shift some or even part of the contract to the healthy spouse via the marital property settlement.

In fact, the annuitant's health decline or severe injury, which occurred sometime after the contract was purchased, is what might have led to the divorce in the first place. The national divorce rate for couples, when one suffers a major chronic illness or permanent disability, shoots through the roof when compared to couples without this additional stressor.

SPIA/DIA Marital Interest—Joint Life

For various reasons, single-life-only DIAs and SPIAs might not be a common purchase for someone who is forty-five and married. A more-common purchase for this relationship dynamic is a spousal joint (JT) with 100 percent survivorship annuity contract. It's common for married annuitants to consider each other's long-term financial interests when making such a purchase.

Payment division and the subsequent contract valuation become muddled because the parties (annuitants) are irrevocable. The payment cannot be divided equally because the survivor annuitant spouse added to the contract at the purchase date was permanent and there was a financial cost to add him or her.

The following table compares how various assets might be divided, highlighting the DIA contracts.

The owner, a fifty-five-year-old male, purchased a joint and 100 percent survivor DIA contract ten years ago with his then spouse, a female, and now age forty-two. At the same time, he also purchased a single-life-only contract for himself. All annuity contracts start their initial payments on his sixty-fifth birthday. In addition, he maintains an investment portfolio. All these assets were acquired during the marriage, utilizing marital property, and these assets are in the marital estate. Also, these assets are to be divided equally. Her interest in the joint and survivor annuity has to be modified because she gets all the survivor benefits as a kind of deferred compensation benefit.

Let's see what this looks like. As of the divorce date, the three assets happen to have values of $100,000 each. In this case, at the time of divorce, the total marital estate was valued at $300,000.

Table (property values at divorce date)

Investment Portfolio	Single Life-Only DIA	JT 100% Life-Only DIA	Annuity Description
$100,000	$100,000	$ 68,859	Life-Only on Him
		$ 31,141	Cost of Her 100% Survivor Benefit
$100,000	$100,000	$100,000	Totals
	$966 - Monthly Payment at His Age 65	$665 – Monthly Payment at His Age 65	

The value of the life-only portion of the joint 100 percent survivor DIA on his life is lower versus his life-only DIA because the monthly payment of $665 is lower than the $966 payment to account for her survivor benefits. Additionally, part of the $100,000 total value of joint life-only DIA represents her survivor benefit. In this example, this amounts to $31,141.

The additional paid premium at the purchase date in order to obtain the 100 percent survivor benefit represents a benefit only she receives because the contract is permanent and her position on the contract as the joint annuitant is irrevocable.

Knowing the above and considering an equal property division, let's look at what a post-divorce property division might look like.

Table (property values post-divorce)

Investment Portfolio	Single Life-Only DIA	JT 100% Life-Only DIA	Annuity Description
$50,000	$100,000	$ 68,859	Life-Only on Him
		$ 31,141	Cost of Her 100% Survivor Benefit
$50,000 (each)	**$100,000** $483(each) - Monthly Payment at His Age 65	**$100,000** $540 (him) $125 (her) Monthly Payment at His Age 65	**Totals**

The investment portfolio is an immediate 50 percent loss. Like I've already said and will say many times in the course of the book, there are many ways to lose money other than in the financial markets. Whatever income would have been generated from that $100,000 portfolio at their joint retirement will never be duplicated with his or her remaining $50,000 post-divorce share.

Let's look at the single-life-only DIA. He will be compelled to give up half of his payment resulting in a post division monthly benefit of $483. But, this benefit terminates when he dies and being he is a male and already thirteen years older than his ex-spouse, this payment is an "ugly" asset relative his ex-wife's financial interests.

The joint 100 percent survivor life-only DIA is little more acceptable to her because she will probably reap a better long-term value because, she gets the entire $665 monthly benefit when he dies. But, why does he get to keep $540 per month now and she only gets $125 per month. It's actually more than he gets to keep on the life-only DIA. What's that all about? How is that fair?

His post-divorce monthly cash flow is better (he gets to put more money in his pocket) with the joint 100 percent Survivor DIA because of her survivor benefit. If the entire annuity value is $100,000 and her share is $50,000 (fifty percent) and since she already receives all the survivorship value of $31,141, her post division value is reduced to $18,859 ($50,000 − $31,141).

Because there is no actual cash, she has to convert her financial interest into a share of the monthly benefit. If her separate property value is $18,859 and the total joint 100 percent Survivor DIA value is $100,000 then, she has a separate property interest of 18.859 percent ($18,859 / $100,000). The monthly payment of $665 times her separate property interest of 18.859 percent means she gets to keep a monthly share of $125 ($665 x 18.8559 percent). He retains the balance $540 ($665 − $125)!

What Might Occur

In reality, because there is a liquid investment portfolio in such cases, rather than completing a division of the annuity payments, a trade proposal might be made. The life-only annuity property interest is really unacceptable for this non-annuitant spouse. An agreement is made that transfers the entire investment portfolio to the ex-wife in exchange for her property claim release in his life-only annuity. Therefore, he now gets to keep the entire $966 monthly benefit.

In a real-life case, a male hard bargainer might offer something less—say, $45,000 (his share) of the portfolio in exchange of the wife's release in his life-only DIA. Otherwise, he could just compel the division of the annuity payment. For her, even though this skews the equal division value, it might be worth a small discount to get some cash and get out of the life-only annuity property interest that doesn't even start paying until ten years from now when his age is sixty-five and she is age fifty-two. In this case, if she accepts his offer, he gets to keep $5,000 of the investment portfolio. She retains $95,000 of the investment portfolio and also signs the property release in his life-only DIA.

In addition to all the above, he inherited property from his mother's estate while they were married, and he did not comingle this property with any marital property. In other words, he took great pains after the inheritance date to keep the property separate. He might just withdraw $18,859 of his own funds and pay his ex-wife her financial interest in the joint 100 percent survivor annuity. In this case, he gets to keep the entire monthly payment of $665 from this contract also.

The end result is annuities, as always, protect income. This is why annuities exist, and in this case he maintains his.

So, in this example, considering the above, what does this all look like? He gets to keep all the monthly annuity income of $1,631 ($966 plus $665) and $5,000 of the investment portfolio value.

She gets a clean break and to keep $113,859—$95,000 of the investment portfolio, plus $18,859 in cash for her property interest in his joint annuity income and the survivorship (deferred compensation) portion of his joint annuity of $665 per month, paid to her at his death. She also has twenty-three more years to her own retirement age of sixty-five, because she is only forty-two now.

But is this a truly fair division? Not really, because the assets are different and are designed to do different things. Only their present dollar values have been dealt with, and they have not been adjusted for risk. His annuity contracts and their incomes are guaranteed by the insurance company. If she attempts to duplicate his initial age sixty-five income at her retirement age sixty-five with her share of the marital estate, she needs to grow the value over the next twenty-three years to about $489,300 in order to reasonably support a monthly withdrawal of $1,631 over her life. Doing so would require her to take significant investment and other risks. She would need to earn roughly 6.50 percent per year during the twenty-three-year deferral period without any other dissipation events and not deviate in her annual withdrawals starting in twenty-three years. In today's financial markets, this rate cannot be achieved by guaranteed investments.

Is she entirely out of luck, though? No, because she could purchase her own lifetime annuity now, with the initial monthly payment starting when she reaches sixty-five. Since she has $113,859 in cash, what kind of an annuity could she purchase? At current annuity rates, her life-only annuity produces a monthly payment of $1,816!

If she adds an annuity purchase refund provision, the payment diminishes to $1,760; if she adds a twenty-year-period certain provision, her payment further diminishes to $1,625. Both the refund and twenty-year-period certain annuity payments provide some estate benefit depending on when she dies. Therefore, she can get the same risk-adjusted benefit, but it requires her to purchase the same kind of property that was previously valued and divided. In real life, would she actually make such a purchase? It's not probable. That would leave her to face the investment and potential dissipation risks, an almost impossible task over such a long duration of twenty-three deferral years and then potentially twenty to twenty-five payment years.

Because there is a thirteen year age difference be-tween her and her ex-husband she can't reasonably expect to see her $665 monthly annuity survivor benefit until she is in her mid-seventies.

It would just be easier and fairer if the insurance company permitted the total withdrawal of his contracts and reissued a new set of contracts to him and to her for each of their separate owner interests from the marital estate. Because of how the contracts are designed, however, this feature will probably never be added.

Reversionary Annuity (RA)—Survivorship
This annuity design is more thoroughly discussed in the "Worlds Collide" chapter. Solely addressing the marital property aspects, the contract is a stand-alone survivorship annuity. The parties to the annuity (the insured and the beneficiary) are irrevocable, and if the contract is paid-up or the insured continues to make the monthly premium payments for this reversionary annuity, the entire annuity value is charged to the spousal beneficiary's side of the property ledger.

So, if the reversionary annuity value is $25,000 to the beneficiary, then $25,000 in other assets needs to be credited to the insured spouse's side of the property ledger (assuming an equal division of assets). Much like a SPIA, the contract is not liquid and has no cash surrender value. Because it is a stand-alone annuity providing the beneficiary only lifetime income and is not associated with a lifetime income on a joint SPIA that pays a lifetime income on two lives, there is no other value to offset against. Therefore, the entire value is charged to the beneficiary as his or her sole property.

Some reversionary annuities have a feature that return paid premiums over a designated period to the insured if the beneficiary happens to predecease the insured. In this case, the insured is a reverse beneficiary. Since only the insured can benefit from this feature, the entire value of this feature needs to be charged against the insured, and assets of equal value need to be credited to the beneficiary.

Because of the actuarial components of a reversionary annuity with both the insured and the beneficiary being medically underwritten by the insurance company to determine annual premium cost for the reversionary annuity payment, the most expensive age/gender combination is a much older male insured with a much younger female beneficiary. However, the reversionary annuity income value is also greater.

As an example, let's consider our case of a male, age sixty-five, and a female, age sixty, that divorce with a reversionary annuity property. The male is the insured and pays a monthly premium of $100 to the insurance company so that upon his death, his soon to be ex-spouse will receive a lifetime $400 monthly annuity payment. At the time of divorce, this reversionary annuity had a current value of about $18,730. In this case, because she gets all reversion annuity value, $18,730 of other property—such as cash or securities—is transferred to him.

Period Certain Payments

Up until this point, we have only discussed life-only and joint life-only annuity contracts. What remains to be considered is a period certain or a cash refund feature. These DIA or SPIA contracts are referred to as period certain and lifetime annuities. Also, some DIAs and SPIAs are exclusively period certain with no lifetime guarantees. The existence of period-certain payments in such contracts doesn't change the method of determining marital interest or the method of valuation because these features can be accounted for in the annuity quotation and pricing process.

If a single annuitant's (e.g., an ex-husband's) certain and lifetime contract becomes divided as to the now separate parties' interest, then each party will probably want to name their own beneficial interests. For example, if I as the nonannuitant spouse (ex-wife), obtain a 25 percent separate property interest share in the monthly income as a result of the property division, I might want to name myself as primary beneficiary for my share and then name my own contingent beneficiary for my share should I predecease the annuitant (ex-husband) and the death benefit becomes payable.

The death benefit might be in the form of a lump sum or a portion of the period-certain payment depending on the DIA or SPIA contract. My contingent beneficiary might be an adult child from another marriage, a parent, a significant other or perhaps even a new spouse.

In this case, prior to the conclusion of the marital property settlement, the annuitant spouse is compelled via the divorce process to irrevocably name me beneficiary and my elected contingent beneficiaries for my 25 percent share. The irrevocable designation here is important because it prevents the annuitant spouse from making any future unilateral beneficiary changes on a post-divorce basis. You just have to make sure the insurance carrier will administrate an irrevocable beneficiary election.

Cost of Living Adjustments (COLAs)

A COLA feature on a SPIA or a DIA contract is merely a way to create an internal deferral. The increase payment in future years is just attributable to the premiums paid to purchase the feature. Therefore, the marital interest in any

COLA is in direct proportion to the marital interest in the paid annuity premium.

The COLA value can be determined in the same manner other contract features are valued by using the replacement cost method previously outlined.

Beneficiaries and Their Own Marriages

One of the beneficiary or even joint annuitant advantages of inheriting a DIA or a SPIA payment is inherited property is specifically exempt from one's marital estate under the UMPA. Since there usually is no cash value but only the payment, there is no chance the beneficiary could later comingle their inheritance or future annuity payments with their own marital estates at a much later date following the inheritance. However, DIAs and SPIAs that offer lump-sum cash payments lose some of this protection. You have to read the contract to determine the beneficiary payment options.

Many a beneficiary has successfully comingled inherited assets in their marital estates —whether they plan to or not. Often there is emotional pressure from the existing spouse to financially support the marriage with joint asset purchases and joint consumption to such a degree these assets and joint consumption cannot be successfully separated as to their separate property inheritance roots at a later date. While the present annuity income payment maybe comingled in such a manner, the future annuity income at any point and time cannot.

The SPIA Contract

It is very important to read the SPIA/DIA contract subject to a marital property claim to determine the contract's operational mechanics. Depending on the contract's features and provisions, it might be easier to physically divide contract values in some contracts and not so easy in others.

For example, some DIA and SPIA contract designs allow for post-issue liquidity features, although this feature may be more prevalent in SPIAs than newer DIA contracts.

After the marital interest has been determined—for example, on a single life SPIA containing period-certain payments—the nonannuitant spouse can compel the annuitant spouse to fully or at least partially commute the contract's payments (if the contract has this feature) to receive their post-division share.

For example, some SPIA designs offer the commutation of all or part of the period-certain payments. If I, the annuitant spouse who is sixty-five, purchase a ten-year period certain and lifetime SPIA (10CL) on my single life; receive payments for two years; and then divorce, the nonannuitant spouse (not wanting anything to do with the annuity) may compel me to commute up to the remaining eight contract years of the period-certain payments to provide the necessary lump-sum value to settle his or her share of the marital estate in this property. If this occurs, I receive no income for the next eight years and only begin to receive my life-only income portion after this time. Also, unfortunately for me, my beneficiary value will be eliminated or perhaps severely reduced.

Multiple Marital Estates

It's not uncommon to find the same asset in more than one marital estate. This is certainly the case for defined benefit plans and 401(k)s. I personally know several individuals who have been married multiple times. Each marital estate has its own distinct claim against the annuity contracts' premium payments made during each respective marital period.

I suspect flexible premium DIAs purchased by individuals ages 30–50, as opposed to traditional SPIAs, will be susceptible to multiple marital estate property claims because the incidence of divorce is higher in the younger age groups. Since the flexible premium DIA is a permanent contract, there are going to be marital property valuation and division issues when multiple marital estates are involved.

If you own a DIA prior to your marriage, it would be best to discontinue paying annual premiums into this contract after your marriage date. Not paying premiums during the marital period will preserve your separate property interest in the contract.

After your marriage date, if you still wanted this kind of contract, it would be better if you purchased a new contract. This contract will become 100% marital property and there will not be any question as to who shares in this interest, since you both will.

If you later become divorced, you can start to make new contributions to your pre-marriage DIA contract or just purchase a new contract. If you follow this pattern, either way, any subsequent new marriage and divorce will keep this property out of your new marital estate.

The DIA premium payment flexibility is a nice advantage you don't have with corporate sponsored retirement plans and many cash value life insurance policies. In these arrangements, you typically have to continue making contributions over the course of your life whether you are married or not. If you go through a divorce, it becomes quite the chore to later separate the marital property from the separate property interests in these arrangements.

Bifurcated Divorce Actions

In some cases, the marital property issues and their values are not entirely clear at the time of divorce. In these cases, some divorcing couples want the divorce to commence as soon as possible so each individual can begin to move on with his or her post-divorce life. To do so, they enter into an agreement to postpone the settlement of all or some of the marital property issues and values to a later date when they may be better determined.

The property-controlling spouse has to act as a "custodian" of the marital estate. They are charged with making reasonable decisions and taking actions so as to not harm the marital estate. Because DIAs and SPIAs are guaranteed irrevocable contracts, except for payment commutation privileges of some SPIAs, the controlling spouse can't dissipate or mismanage the contracts as they can with other forms of property such as investment portfolios, businesses, rental properties, retirement plans, etc.

The one thing to keep in mind is the life contingent DIA value will potentially rise and fall on the future death or any adverse health change of the annuitant spouse. An annuitant deferral period death may terminate the DIA contract without further value. If the annuitant spouse becomes injured or contracts cancer or HIV or develops some other life-threatening disease, before or even after the annuity commencement date, the value of the DIA or even SPIA will be significantly reduced.

Death or Incapacity of the Ex-Spouse and Marital Estate Claims

There is always the potential for the death or incapacity of the nonannuitant spouse either during the deferral period or after the annuity payment commencement date. Nonannuitants may die, but marital estates do not.

One of the risks individuals run into with a bifurcated divorce action where some or all of the marital property issues are settled at a later date is the ex-spouse may die or become incapacitated prior to reaching a final marital property settlement.

While an opportunity for an amicable settlement might have existed while the ex-spouse was alive, marital property settlements can quickly turn acrimonious when having to deal with the beneficiaries of the marital estate. These beneficiaries are usually children from the marriage, children from a prior marriage or perhaps siblings and parents of the ex-spouse.

Since the relationship dynamics are much different between children and in-laws than parting spouses, the marital property settlement process can become quite the nightmare—particularly when being forced to deal with these nonspousal individuals who have a financial interest in the marital estate.

The classic scenario involves adult children of the marriage or a prior marriage of the deceased spouse who have an existing acrimonious relationship with their father or stepfather, depending on the case. Dad divorced their mother only to remarry someone the kids don't like. Due to Mom's death or incapacitation, the kids now have a financial interest in Mom's post-divorce marital estate and are calling all the settlement shots with Dad.

Just as in all family matters that entwine money and emotion, the larger the marital estate, the bigger the potential disputes and the larger the legal fees to resolve outstanding issues among warring parties.

The QDRO versus DRO Process

The legal document that actually divides the marital interest in qualified retirement plans into separate property interests is the qualified domestic relations order (QDRO). However, by definition, neither an IRA DIA nor a SPIA is a qualified retirement plan. An IRA is defined as an "individual retirement arrangement" and as such, like other personal or real property, is divided by a domestic relations order (DRO).

A QDRO is subject to various rules that establish parameters about its contents and language. QDROs are also reviewed by the institution holding the qualified plan both for language and to determine any plan conflicts for approval prior to the QDRO submission to the court for the final judgment.

Because a DRO has no such preapproval requirement, many divorcing parties and their counsel fail to fully consider the basis and all the features of the IRA DIA, SPIA or other nonqualified annuity. This may result in problems long after contract division or disposition when it is too late to adequately readdress them.

The DIA and SPIA contract illiquidity—as with other financial products, such as employee pensions and other deferred compensation—may set up tough decision making on the parts of both spouses as they grapple with just how fair an economic settlement may be reached considering the long-term financial interests of each spouse.

A DIA, SPIA or even a reversionary annuity could be in force for decades, as they typically have no surrender value. Each spouse must decide about the disposition of their separate property share within the best possible light, at the time of divorce.

Chapter Summary
• SPIAs and DIAs are illiquid financial products and receive special considerations when they fall into marital estates stemming from divorce.

• The Uniform Marital Property Act (UMPA) promulgated by the Uniform Law Commissioners in 1983 provides the basis for determining what is and is not marital property.

• Since SPIAs and DIAs have very few moving parts and can't typically be altered after the contract issue date, it's imperative to review the contract to determine who the parties are and who gets which benefit.

• Typically, SPIAs and DIAs provided better consumer protection, preserving contract values for both parties in a divorce versus more liquid forms of property that can easily become dissipated in the asset division process.

• Bifurcated divorce actions can produce unintended outcomes relating to SPIA and DIA contracts. Long settlement times may expose the parties to changing health circumstances and capacities needed to reap full contract values.

• The legal document dividing the marital interest in an IRA or even a non-IRA DIA or SPIA is a domestic relations order (DRO). The DRO should be carefully reviewed by an expert in the property being divided. The more commonly known legal document is a qualified domestic relations order (QDRO), but it is only used for qualified retirement plan dispositions.

End Notes

Elliot, Diana B. and Tavia Simmons. "Marital Events of Americans: 2009." United States Census Bureau: United States Department of Commerce, August 2011.

Mettler, Gary S. "Oh No! DIAs and SPIAs in Marital Property Estates." White Paper, December 2011.

THIRD PARTIES

"In the fields of Hell where the grass grows high
are there graves of dreams allowed to die."
—*Richard Harter, poet*

Introduction

I am not a fan of third-party organizations that purchase SPIA payments from individuals. Many refer to this group of companies as a "secondary market"; however, "market" is an overly generous term. I believe when consumers hear the word "market," they get this impression of some active exchange like the stock market, made up of thousands of buyers and sellers at any given minute.

Third-party SPIA marketers are really a loose confederation of predominantly unregulated firms. With the exception of a few companies, most jump in and out of business. Their employees are not required to be licensed by any federal or state authority. These firms' operations are more closely aligned with the "factoring industry." This is an industry that usually provides a financing method through which a business owner sells accounts receivable at a discount to a third-party funding source to raise capital. But other types of steady cash flows, such as payments from immediate annuities can be sold as well.

Role

Third parties have flitted around the SPIA industry for several decades. These companies stand ready to purchase SPIA payments from consumers who, after buying a SPIA, decide for one reason or another to sell all or some of their future payments for cash today. It started in the structured settlement industry, in which plaintiffs who were awarded or settled their lawsuit cases for SPIA contracts (structured settlements) attempted to later sell some or all their payments. Initially, there was an income tax cloud over structured settlement sales transactions, but later income tax laws were modified to remove possible adverse income tax ramifications.

Typically a consumer in tough financial straits might turn to the SPIA factoring industry as a last resort to sell some or all their SPIA payments. This might entail a broker—not necessarily an insurance agent—contacting one or two firms with an offer to sell payments from one of his or her clients. These firms, knowing the financial straits such a consumer may be in, are not too generous with their purchase terms. It's kind of like going to a pawn broker to sell your jewelry. You know you will get something for it but nowhere near what you paid for it.

What's more, if you have only one or two offers to buy payments, there are going to be pricing discrepancies; because there are not many factoring firms lining-up to purchase these payments.

Also, because of the nature of the transaction, your selling costs will be high. Many sellers also use the services of an attorney, which I highly recommend, if you engage in this kind of a transaction. SPIA contracts, because they are illiquid, have all kinds of property issues that need to be addressed. Usually the contract title (ownership) passes to the purchasing party, because income tax reporting goes to SPIA owners. Sellers don't want to pay income tax on payments they will no longer receive as a result of the sale.

Period Certain-Only Complete Sale
If I receive a $1,000 monthly payment from a 120-month (ten-year) period-certain-only contract, for a total of $120,000 of guaranteed payments, I might sell the entire contract and receive a $95,000 lump sum. The buyer will become the new owner with a tax basis (their cost to purchase) and receive the contract gains over ten years. The buyer then controls all aspects of the contract. The buyer names themselves the beneficiary in case I die during this 120-month period. Per the contract, I remain the annuitant because that can't be changed by the new owner. If I die during this annuity period, a death benefit—in this case, any future remaining payments—is paid to the contract purchaser, the new beneficiary.

If my $95,000 proceeds are less than my remaining contract basis, then I can deduct the loss accordingly (see "Tax Implications" chapter). If the $95,000 proceeds are more than my remaining cost basis in the contract, then I will have an ordinary taxable gain.

Period Certain-Only Partial Sale
A partial sale of the same contract is more complicated than a full sale. I decide to sell only $400, or 40 percent, of my $1,000 monthly payment and instead receive a $38,000 lump sum. Because of income tax reporting, the contract title (ownership) still goes to the purchaser. However, I need a side agreement to re-allow me $600 per month for 120 months as part of the SPIA payment I retained. Perhaps the insurance carrier will agree to split the payment and directly

pay me the $600 monthly income. However, in this case, I would need an agreement to compel the purchaser to make my payee status irrevocable. In addition, I need an agreement that will permit me to name my own beneficiary and make beneficiary changes for my $600 monthly benefit. Again, checking with the insurance company, the company may accommodate my beneficiary nomination on an irrevocable basis. All terms must be irrevocable because the new owner, the purchaser of the payments, needs to be prohibited from making changes that affect my remaining payments after the sale transaction date. This is why you need an attorney to help review all the sales documentation.

What about income taxes? Chances are the purchaser of the SPIA payments will report the entire purchase—in this case $38,000—as 1099 income (taxable income) to you the seller, but is this correct? What about your $600 share of the monthly income paid to you by the purchaser—how should you report it? When you owned the annuity contract, you received income tax reporting by the insurance company according to the SPIA tax rules. In any given year, part of the income was taxable, and part was not taxable.

The purchasers of such SPIA contracts will not give you income tax reporting advice because it isn't their problem. Probably the best way to deal with the $38,000 lump-sum income tax issue is to use the "cream in coffee" rule (see "Tax Implications" chapter). If you sold 40 percent of the payment, then 40 percent of the remaining tax basis at the time of sale also went to the purchaser. Your tax preparer may wish to use a different tax reporting method.

If the annuity tax basis prior to the sale was $90,000, the buyer gets $36,000 (40 percent of $90,000), and you retain $54,000. In this treatment, you report a $2,000 ordinary taxable gain for the lump-sum payment of $38,000 ($38,000 minus $36,000). For your future income payments of $600 per month, you still have $54,000 of tax basis to use. The tax basis per month you get to utilize in this example is $450 ($54,000 over 120 months). If your monthly income remains at $600, then only $150 ($600 minus $450) per month is taxable.

But you are going to have to explain all this to the IRS and document what happened so they understand how you elected to treat the transaction for income tax reporting purposes.

Period Certain and Lifetime Sale
The first two examples were for period-certain-only SPIAs. What if the SPIA also has some life-contingent payments, such as period certain for ten years followed by lifetime payments? This will almost always result in a partial sale because most third-party buyers will not purchase lifetime contingent payments, thinking of them as too risky to permit them a proper return on their capital.

Once the period-certain duration was sold completes, the contract ownership should revert back to the annuitant who sold the payments so he or she may start collecting payments once again from the insurance company. Any remaining period-certain duration and lifetime benefits should be made from the insurance company. However, because part of the contract was sold and tax basis reported changed, the insurance company will not have the correct remaining tax basis information and will most likely be reluctant to change their records. Because of this, the consumer will once again have to provide the adjusted cost basis for income tax calculations to the IRS for the remaining life of the contract.

IRA SPIA Sale

What if a SPIA is also an IRA? For IRAs, the tax treatment is questionable. By law, only the IRA holder of the contract can be the owner of the contract, so the purchaser of IRA-SPIA payments cannot become the new contract owner. The purchasers claim they are not lenders (loans using IRAs as collateral are also not permitted) but merely purchasing future payments at a discount. The IRA holder still retains ownership and pays income tax on the SPIA payments as they are received. After payments are received in this manner, the SPIA owner just simply sends the payment or part of the payment, depending on the amount sold, to the purchaser according to their contractual agreement.

The IRS has been looking at this, and it's not clear how they will treat it. The feeling is this "purchase" is really a de facto loan in disguise; if so, the entire lump sum should be treated as taxable income as a withdrawal. Until the IRS clears this up, it's better to stay away from factoring IRA SPIA payments.

SPIA Death Claims Sale

Owners are one thing, and beneficiaries are another. When SPIA owners die after electing period-certain-only and period-certain and life contracts, and if the entire period-certain duration was not complete, contract beneficiaries will collect the remaining unpaid payments. For example, if I purchased a fifteen-year period-certain and life SPIA and died after five years, my beneficiaries collect the scheduled payments for ten more years. In this example, if my beneficiary was my estate, the estate would have to stay open for ten years in order to collect all the payments and pay any income tax due.

Without a SPIA commutation privilege (see below), I as the estate trustee or beneficiary may not want to wait ten years to get these payments and instead turn to a third party to purchase them from me. Again, I would be subject to the same sales conditions, with purchasers knowing I really don't want the payments and might be willing to entertain any "reasonable" offer—the pawn shop experience.

As a death claim, there is no contract to transfer because the contract privileges end with the death of the annuitant or owner, depending on the contract. I might end up having to still receive payments and then just sending them to the purchaser through a contractual agreement. If the carrier permitted, I could just instruct them to send the payments to a third-party payee. However, income tax reporting by the carrier to me would still continue because tax liability for the payment cannot be so transferred. I would then have to explain to the IRS every year about the tax reporting inconsistencies. Because of this, I don't recommend a death claim sale of annuity payments.

SPIA Payment Commutations

As outlined in the "Variability" chapter, a SPIA commutation is a contractual provision or rider attached to the SPIA contract by the insurance company that permits SPIA owners and sometimes beneficiaries to withdrawal or at least partially withdrawal payment rights depending on the contract. This is done by "commutating" future monthly payments back to lump-sum amounts. This is accomplished by a rider (a mini-agreement/contract) or specific annuity features, if by rider the rider has to be added to the contract at the SPIA purchase date.

The really good thing about SPIAs with these features versus third-party sales is commutation costs and methods of calculation are established by the contract. Consumers no longer have to rely on shadowy and unregulated third parties to establish uncompetitive market sales terms.

The other good thing is carriers will consider the "cream in coffee" rule when reporting the cash lump-sum taxable amount and the new taxable portion of the future remaining payments, correctly reporting all to the IRS for consumer convenience.

Not all carriers offer SPIAs with commutation features. On the other hand, SPIA commutation features take away some of the safety elements (see "Protection" chapter), and the SPIA tax treatment concerning the remaining SPIA contract is not too clear—although the IRS had a chance to address it when they ruled on SPIA withdrawals but either elected not to address the "substantially equal payment" issue of the remaining payments of the contract or they just didn't consider the remaining payment issue.

Chapter Summary
• Selling future SPIA payments to third parties is a transaction fraught with legal and income tax difficulties. The third-party annuity purchase industry is not well regulated, and its sales representatives are typically not licensed. However, if you are compelled to approach a third party to purchase future SPIA payments, it is wise to incorporate the services of an experienced attorney in these matters.

• Third-party sales typically incorporate transfer of ownership rights to the third-party purchaser, so you might need supporting legal agreements that permit you to retain certain rights, like beneficiary changes and bank-payee privileges.

• Because of how the premium cost basis may be allocated between the seller and the third-party purchaser, income tax issues can become complicated. A complete sale of a period-certain-only contract provides an easier income tax reporting event. However, partial sales of such contracts (or of those that also incorporate life-contingent payments) can cause income tax reporting problems.

• Until the IRS rules on how sales of SPIA payments from IRA contracts will be treated, it is best to avoid these transactions. As a SPIA owner, if you think you may need future lump sums from your contract, you can purchase a SPIA contract that offers full or partial payment commutations. However, this will cost you some of the protection elements of the contract in the form of lost anti-dissipation benefits.

PRETENDERS TO THE THRONE

**"There are pretenders to piety
as well as to courage."**
—*Moliere, French playwright*

Introduction

In all kingdoms, there are pretenders and challengers to the throne. In the annuity income world this challenge comes from a closely related cousin, the deferred annuity. Going back to the "History" and "Agent" chapters, agents for various reasons are often more comfortable presenting deferred annuities with withdrawal features that mimic the annual income produced by a SPIA. One of the primary comfort reasons is deferred annuity contracts are viewed by the agent and consumers as an investment; they are not too comfortable with all the insurance aspects of a SPIA. For years, much of the annuity agent training has been focused on investment-type implications and not on insurance implications. Due to lack of financial product education, consumers also struggle with viewing annuity contracts as insurance products.

To this end, carriers started to develop withdrawal guarantees for variable, fixed and fixed index (a type of fixed contract) deferred annuity contracts. They are often referred to as guaranteed lifetime withdrawal benefits (GLWBs) for fixed contracts and guaranteed withdrawal benefits (GWBs) for variable annuity contracts. While this book does not go into a discussion of variable annuity contracts, it will touch on fixed index annuity contracts only to the extent necessary to review this particular income guarantee.

The Guarantee

The basic framework for the income withdrawal guarantee is for the consumer to purchase the deferred contract with some single or even multiple premiums. Then, after the contract issue date, usually after a period of several years, depending on the contract, consumers have the option to start contract withdrawals at some fixed rate tied to a formula. As long as the contract stays in force and the consumer abides by the terms of the formula established by the contract, the contract guarantees to continue the withdrawal rate even if the contract's cash value reduces to zero.

I prefer to call these "provisional" guarantees. The result, if all goes well, is a lifetime income guarantee, with some ifs. Even with all life's uncertainties, sales of this type of annuity guarantee is the most popular today, breathing life into the depressed annuity industry caused by low interest rates. Agents and the industry cavalierly refer to these features as a "lifetime income guarantee" because they don't take into account possible post issue hurdles consumers might face that would cause the consumer to diminish this guarantee by making large cash withdrawals or just plain lapsing the contract. In other words, these guarantees only work if consumers play by the rules established by the contract. If they break the contract rules, they may suffer a diminished guarantee or an outright loss of the guarantee if they are compelled or even elect to surrender the contract. That's why I call them provisional guarantees. Promising a guarantee with strings attached is not really a guarantee.

Sequence of Returns Risk

What's more, scheduling fixed annual withdrawals from guaranteed cash-value annuity contracts has the added benefit of providing a reliable and stable-value source of funds, because the insurance company guarantees the actual cash values from day to day. This makes comparisons easier. While it is not covered in this book, an additional problem with this same income-withdrawal schedule occurs when a fund's source—say, stocks and bonds or other market-adjusted securities in an investment portfolio—can advance or decline in value on any given day. Portfolio-value declines occurring at the same time as scheduled annual withdrawals can severely impact the investment portfolio's longevity and its ability to support long-term, scheduled withdrawals. This is known as the "sequence of returns risk."

Here's an example of sequence of returns risk: your investment portfolio is $100,000, and you calculate a 5 percent annual withdrawal rate (or $5,000) to support a twenty-year withdrawal scheme (ignoring gains). After your withdrawal, if the portfolio value subsequently declines to $50,000 due to stock and bond market value fluctuations, you will be compelled to reduce your annual withdrawal rate the following year to $2,631 ($50,000 divided by nineteen years) to make your money last. If you failed to adjust your annual withdrawal and there were no further market value changes (ignoring gains and additional losses), your withdrawal period would be reduced to just ten years ($50,000 at $5,000 per year). Surviving this period with a zero account balance, you would have no more funds to withdraw.

Many investment advisors incorporate fixed deferred annuity contracts as well as immediate annuity contracts with investment portfolios to ease this risk, leaving you annuity income resources in case you experience negative financial market results after you start to make investment portfolio withdrawals.

The Guarantee Mechanics

Typically, a two-part formula determines the annual lifetime income guarantee, which is usually paid monthly. The first part is a simple percentage rate or withdrawal rate—4 to 6 percent (not an earnings rate) or more per year depending on the owner's age at the time the withdrawal commences. The second part of the formula is the "withdrawal value" this percentage is applied against. The withdrawal value is not the same thing as the contract's cash value. The withdrawal value is a contrived number, according to a formula, outlined in the contract by the carrier. As a beginning basis of calculating the withdrawal value, the carrier might use a number equal to the premium paid plus some bonus amount and some annual interest rate to continuously grow the withdrawal value. This withdrawal value can only be realized by making the scheduled annual withdrawals. See the example below.

For withdrawal value calculation purposes only, a person age sixty purchases a deferred annuity with a GLWB with an initial premium of $100,000 combined with a $5,000 bonus amount growing at 6.00 percent per year. In this case, the withdrawal value will be $140,514 after five years. For a person age sixty-five, the withdrawal percentage rate is 5.50 percent. Therefore, the lifetime annual income guarantee is $7,728.00 or about $644.00 monthly.

Annuity with GLWB – Formula

Premium (Tax Basis)	Bonus	Total	5-Year Withdrawal Value At 6.00%	Withdrawal Rate	Annual Income Guarantee
$100,000	$5,000	$105,000	$140,514	5.50%	$7,728

Of course, if the actual cash value due to earnings has increased to more than $140,514, then this number will be used to determine the annual income. Withdrawals reduce the cash value, as well as the withdrawal value determined by the formula. In addition, there is usually an annual expense charge for this feature of about 1.00 percent, depending on the contract, that works to also reduce the contracts actual cash value.

If the contracts earnings rate can't keep up with the withdrawal rate and contract expenses, the actually cash value will slowly diminish over the course of several years. Because of this, while the income is high relative to the withdrawal value, consumers typically sacrifice the contract's death benefit, because the death benefit is usually the remaining actual cash value of the contract. Some contracts permit a death benefit based on the remaining withdrawal value if taken over a period of years, or some percentage of the withdrawal value is taken as a lump sum. In this scenario, you are receiving a relatively high income but at the expense of your death benefit.

Of course, if the deferred contract performs exceedingly well by crediting a high level of earnings, you could end up with a good income and a growing death benefit. However, using the contract in our example, the contract earnings would have to exceed 6.00 percent per year plus an additional 1.00 percent to cover the contract expense for a total of 7.00 percent for that to occur.

Another difference is the income tax treatment of the deferred annuity contract withdrawal. Withdrawals from deferred annuity contracts are income taxable to the extent of the gains in the contract. Using our example contract, the actual cash value after five years—including the bonus amount of $5,000 and assuming an annual 3.00 percent earnings rate—is $121,723 (assume the $5,000 bonus is vested in the actual cash value). The actual constant earnings rate on the cash value is different than the rate applied for income value determination. This rate is set by the contract formula.

Annuity with GLWB - Cash Value

Premium (Tax Basis)	Bonus	Total	5-Year Actual Cash Value at 3.00%	Cash Withdrawal Annual Rate	Cash Balance After Withdrawal
$100,000	$5,000	$105,000	$121,723	$7,728	$113,995

The contract tax basis is $100,000, because that was the actual premium paid. The accumulated gain is $21,723. A withdrawal after five years of $7,728 is 100 percent taxable because deferred annuity withdrawals have to come from gains first. Of course, from the SPIA discussion in the taxation chapter, SPIA income is partially taxable and partially nontaxable according to the IRS table for that particular SPIA.

Systematic Withdrawal

A close relative to the deferred annuity with a GLWB feature is a fixed deferred annuity placed on an easy-to-understand systematic withdrawal for a lifetime income strategy. While a GLWB feature and a systematic withdrawal are the same thing for tax purposes, a systematic withdrawal is perhaps easier to understand because it uses no formula and has no contract expenses. Also, deferred annuities with GLWB features use more complex methods to determine earnings, such as links to various stock and bond market indices versus traditional fixed annuities that credit fixed interest earnings.

Using the same example, an individual age sixty purchases a traditional, fixed-interest, crediting deferred annuity for $100,000 (no bonus amount) and can obtain a rate of 2.50 percent for five years. At age sixty-five, this contract's cash value is $113,141. Assuming a withdrawal rate of 5.00 percent, or $5,657, per year and a constant earnings rate of 2.50 percent (guaranteed by the contract), this contract will reduce to $0 value after twenty-seven years, at age ninety-two. Under these assumptions, the annuity with the GLWB feature actually runs out of cash value before the traditional fixed annuity on a systematic withdrawal.

Systematic Withdrawal Cash Value

Premium (Tax Basis)	5-Year Actual Cash Value at 2.50%	Cash Withdrawal Annual Rate	Cash Balance After Withdrawal	Cash Balance at Age 92
$100,000	$113,141	$5,657	$107,484	$0

Vs.

Annuity with GLWB - Cash Value

Premium (Tax Basis) with Bonus	5-Year Actual Cash Value at 3.00%	Cash Withdrawal Annual Rate	Cash Balance After Withdrawal	Cash Balance at Age 87
$105,000	$121,723	$7,728	$113,995	$0

I made allowances for a 20 percent increase of the earnings rate to 3.00 percent for the annuity with the GLWB feature over the 2.50 percent earnings rate of the traditional fixed annuity. Since annuities with GLWB feature utilize external indices to calculate interest earnings, I assumed these contracts might produce constantly higher earnings over time versus a fixed deferred annuity declared interest rate contract. The fact the deferred annuity with the GLWB feature runs out of cash value first makes sense, because the withdrawal amount is so much larger relative to its cash value versus the withdrawal amount of the fixed annuity without the GLWB feature. Actually, these results are skewed because I didn't incorporate the internal cost—typically about 1.00 percent per year—for having a GLWB feature. Since this cost reduces cash value over time, the annuity with the GLWB feature cash value will give out sooner than age eighty-seven.

The difference is even if the annuity with the GLWB feature has a $0 cash value, as long as you played by the contract rules and didn't lapse the contract, the carrier still needs to make the income payment. This is the protection you receive in exchange for the annual 1.00 percent expense.

Typically, once the cash value is gone, the death benefit is also gone. Some annuity contracts with GLWB features might pay the highest amount among the cash value, the income value, or the remaining part of the income value (after subtracting withdrawals) used in the formula to determine the annual income amount when death occurs. This might be in the form of a lump sum or some short duration annuity.

However, the GLWB annuity income value of $140,514 reduces to $0 under an annual withdrawal rate of $7,728 at age eighty-three. At least in this example, the income value reduces to $0 before the actual cash value does.

Because of this, in a way, once you begin withdrawals, you are robbing Peter to pay Paul. You're stepping up your current income at the expense of reducing the contract's legacy value for your beneficiaries toward $0.

In order to make these comparisons of GLWB income versus systematic withdrawal income, I had to make a few assumptions given the set of facts. One of the biggest assumptions is the deferred annuity with the GLWB feature and the deferred annuity with interest crediting earn set annual rates of 3.00 percent and 2.50 percent respectively. The reality is it's highly unlikely this will be the case over so many withdrawal decades. I elected these rates to reflect current rates typically available for these contracts at the time of writing.

If earnings increase over the decades, the contracts would not run out of cash value, and they may retain some death benefit to age one hundred and beyond.

SPIA

One of my favorite SPIA examples of current income combined with a legacy benefit is a joint SPIA contract incorporating a parent with a survivor payment made to a son or daughter. Let's look at two cases: a joint and survivor 100 percent and a joint and survivor 50 percent payment. Both payment schedules are common and can be purchased from most SPIA carriers. This means the entire payment is made to the parent, and then, at the parent's death, either 100 or 50 percent of the payment goes to the child, depending on the case. Both the parent and the child are in the carrier's mortality pool, so this becomes a permanent contract. This SPIA has many post issue benefits versus a deferred annuity with a GLWB feature or on a systematic withdrawal schedule.

Let's look at some SPIA incomes with current rates. A father is age sixty-five, and his son is age forty at the time of purchase. The same premiums to purchase the SPIA are used in the above examples—$113,141 for the fixed annuity on systematic withdrawal and $121,723 for the annuity with the GLWB feature to determine the SPIA annual income. Let's see the tables below.

Joint SPIA Income with Son vs. Fixed Deferred Annuity Systematic Withdrawal

SPIA Premium (Cost Basis)	Dad's Annual Income 100% Survivor to Son	Dad's Annual Income 50% Survivor to Son	Son's 50% Survivor Benefit	Fixed Annuity Annual Systematic Withdrawal
$113,141	$5,160	$6,012	$3,006	$5,657

Joint SPIA Income with Son vs. Deferred Annuity with GLWB Feature Withdrawal

SPIA Premium (Cost Basis)	Dad's Annual Income 100% Survivor to Son	Dad's Annual Income 50% Survivor to Son	Son's 50% Survivor Benefit	Fixed Annuity Annual GLWB Feature
$121,723	$5,556	$6,468	$3,234	$7,728

First, let's consider the income tax. The SPIA income is taxed with about 51 percent and 67 percent excluded from income tax for the 100 percent and the 50 percent survivor benefit to the son, respectively. This excluded portion continues until the entire cost basis is reduced to $0. At this rate, the excluded portion will continue to Dad's age 108 for the 100 percent survivor benefit and until he is age 96 and 6 months for the 50 percent survivor benefit. Remember, any withdrawals from the tax deferred annuities are taxed from gains first. Depending on your income tax rate, the SPIA could produce more after tax income.

Dad's current income for the 50 percent survivor payment to his son is higher than his income from the 100 percent survivor payment to his son. This makes sense because Dad, being twenty-five years older than his son, is more likely actuarially to predecease his son. The insurance company can pay Dad more current income because when Dad dies, his son's payment becomes 50 percent—$3,006 or $3,234, depending on the premium cost above.

For the 100 percent survivor benefit income, the tax beauty is the excluded amount Dad enjoys stays the same when the son inherits (see below). For example, the excluded amounts for the $113,141 and the $121,723 contracts are $2,632 and $2,834 respectively. Dad's excluded amounts for the 50 percent survivor benefit income are $4,028 and $4,334 respectively. Because son's payments are reduced by fifty percent at Dad's death his excluded amounts are also reduced to $2,014 and $2,167 respectively

This continues until all the premium cost is completely recovered. After that, the son pays income tax on the entire annual income. He inherits the same tax benefit his dad had, making this a very income tax-efficient inheritance

Joint SPIA Income with Son vs. Fixed Deferred Annuity Systematic Withdrawal

SPIA Premium (Cost Basis)	Dad's Annual Income 100% Survivor to Son	Dad's Excluded Portion 51% From Income Tax	Dad's Annual Income 50% Survivor to Son	Dad's Excluded Portion 67% From Income Tax	Annual Systematic Withdrawal Income 100% Taxable
$113,141	$5,160	$2,632	$6,012	$4,028	$5,657

Joint SPIA Income with Son vs. Deferred Annuity with GLWB Feature Withdrawal

SPIA Premium (Cost Basis)	Dad's Annual Income 100% Survivor to Son	Dad's Excluded Portion 67% From Income Tax	Dad's Annual Income 50% Survivor to Son	Dad's Excluded Portion 67% From Income Tax	Annual GLWB Withdrawal Income 100% Taxable
$121,723	$5,556	$2,834	$6,468	$4,334	$7,728

With the joint and survivor SPIA, there will always be an inheritance, assuming the parent survives to a normal life expectancy and predeceases the child, who also survives to a normal life expectancy

Let's assume Dad survives to age eighty-five, and the son inherits the payment at age sixty. Recalling there is a twenty-five-year age difference, let's assume the son survives to age eighty-seven. Who got what?

What Dad Received

Annuity	Dads Age 85 Total Received Income at Death 100% Survivor Annuity (For 20 Years)	Dads Age 85 Total Received Income at Death 50% Survivor Annuity (For 20 Years)
$113,141	$103,200	$120,240
$121,723	$111,120	$129,360

What Son Received

Annuity	Sons Age 60 Total Received Income at Death Age 87 100% Survivor Annuity (For 27 Years)	Sons Age 60 Total Received Income at Death Age 87 50% Survivor Annuity (For 27 Years)
$113,141	$139,320	$81,162
$121,723	$150,012	$87,318

With this SPIA there are no moving parts. It's simple and very easy to understand; the longer each survives the more money each receives.

Tallying Up the Benefits

Deferred Annuity Contracts
For deferred annuities, as long as you manage the withdrawals, you might achieve a lifetime income objective for yourself. You certainly have access to the cash values if you are in dire need of a withdrawal, and while this may damage your guarantees and or the ability of the contract to support withdrawals over your lifetime, the cash is there. Your beneficiaries may inherit some lump-sum value with the option of purchasing their own annuity at your death. This depends on contract performance and your withdrawals. Withdrawals are subject to income tax from contract gains first.

Immediate Annuity
This is a much simpler arrangement because you don't have to manage withdrawals or be concerned with contract earnings. While there is no cash access (at least in this example, because some SPIA contracts do have cash access in the form of commuted payments), due to the

IRS-permitted excluded portion, the income tax benefits are typically superior because your after-tax income may be higher. Both you and your beneficiary receive lifetime incomes. This particular SPIA has more staying power in the face of consumer adversity than the deferred cash value contracts. Long after contracts are purchased and issued by the carriers, problematic post purchase events can occur that threaten deferred contract ownership. Since this SPIA has no cash value, it can't become displaced or dissipated, and the son who is a joint annuitant can't become removed. Anyone living an unsheltered life knows typically unpredictable stuff just happens.

SPIAs purchased at age sixty-five will not be included in Dad's Medicaid estate for long-term care purposes at age eighty-seven. While the annuity income will be counted, the premium cost to purchase the annuity in this case will not be counted. If Dad has to do a bankruptcy because of a business failure or a major casualty loss, the SPIA will be protected to some extent from creditors, depending on the state, and from litigants seeking financial damages. If Dad becomes ill or injured and is compelled to turn his financial affairs over to another, such as a sibling or even an adult child, the SPIA assures Dad's income continues without interference. If there is sibling rivalry at Dad's illness, no one dominating sibling with a power of attorney or conservatorship for Dad can, in this case, remove another sibling from Dad's contract. When the son inherits Dad's annuity income, it can never become part of his marital estate. Deferred cash value annuities just fall short of protecting their owners and beneficiaries from these life events and others.

Chapter Summary

• Many agents and consumers seeking income may use deferred annuity contracts with new secondary guarantees: guaranteed lifetime withdrawal benefit (GLWB) for fixed contracts and guaranteed withdrawal benefit (GWB) for variable annuity contracts, or traditional systematic withdrawal features of deferred annuity contracts. Often these benefits are realized at the expense of the contracts' death benefit, which is undermined by diminishing cash values.

• The annuity contract mechanics of using secondary guarantees is convoluted at best, confusing consumers and agents alike. They create additional costs, diminishing the deferred annuity cash value. A systematic withdrawal may be a better choice versus GLWBs and GWBs; internal costs are lower, and contracts are easier to manage. Unlike investment portfolios composed of variable-price assets such as stocks and bonds, fixed deferred annuities and SPIAs both avoid the sequence of returns risk that damages investment portfolios when consumers make scheduled withdrawals in declining markets.

• When the IRS-permitted exclusion ratio is used, SPIA income tax advantages are superior to the gains-out-first taxation imposed on deferred annuity withdrawals. SPIA owners, joint annuitants and beneficiaries all benefit from exclusion ratio treatment.

• Overall, the SPIA has more staying power because consumers can't lapse the contract by choice or be compelled to surrender it, unlike deferred annuity contracts. SPIAs remain in force over longer durations, producing dependable income.

WORLDS COLLIDE

**"If you change the way you look at things,
the things you look at change."**
—*Wayne Dyer, psychologist*

Introduction

Since about 2008, the states permitted the annuity industry to reintroduce a fixed and deferred immediate annuity contract for sales to retail consumers. While these contracts are called deferred immediate by actuaries, they are often referred to as deferred income annuity (DIA) contracts by agents and the consumer financial press. It is somewhat confusing to consumers to call something deferred and immediate in the same breath. But let's recall our definition of an immediate annuity. An immediate annuity is defined by its pricing date and not by its payment date. An immediate annuity priced now but happens to have a long initial payment deferral period starting from the purchase date, from one year to thirty years prior to the payment commencement date, is commonly referred to as a DIA.

To get the gist of what a DIA does, I often use the following analogy. As you start your career, you are at the foot of a high mountain, at the top of which is your retirement plateau. You have to reach this plateau by running up a perilous system of mountain trails. Along this run, you gather water in buckets you have to carry if you want to have some water to drink when you get there. The problem is the trails are steep and rocky, and the climate is hot. You stumble, and some water spills. You get thirsty and drink some along the way. A predator attacks you and takes some water. By the time you eventually reach the mountaintop, you may not have too much water left. What a DIA does is say, *Hey, don't worry about your water; when you get to the top of the mountain, it will be there waiting for you.*

For a DIA, there is nothing to manage after the purchase date; the consumer merely receives a contract for the specified guaranteed payment. If the contract permits multiple premium payments, the consumer receives a statement indicating what the new cumulative annual income (usually expressed as a monthly income) will be on the payment date. The contract is typically purchased at about age forty or fifty and features initial payment dates from age sixty to sixty-five. That's it; it's just that simple.

The entire DIA contract averages eight to fifteen pages compared to their modern-day fixed or variable deferred annuity behemoth cousins that often push forty to eighty dizzying pages. DIA contracts are elegant in their simplicity.

Deferred Immediate/Deferred Income Annuity (DIA)
From about the late 1970s up until this time—roughly the last forty years or so—deferred annuity contracts were known primarily as savings devices to which the consumer made contributions that earned some fixed interest rate or were invested in the financial markets. While deferred annuity contracts have the option of converting to SPIAs, most contract owners make elections to surrender them either fully or partially over time when they want the deferred annuity contracts' proceeds. I don't cover deferred

annuity contracts in this book except to demonstrate how they relate to SPIAs. Also, I explored deferred annuity contracts somewhat in the "Pretenders to the Throne" chapter.

Starting at the beginning of the twenty first century there were few prescient individuals who foresaw a possible time in which interest rates could fall to unprecedented lows and take years to fully recover to normal levels. A DIA uses both interest and mortality to price annuity payments.

What makes these contracts so impressive from a pricing perspective? There are several factors. One factor is the contract is permanent; since consumers don't have elective withdrawal features, insurance carriers can invest differently and for longer durations. This type of investing usually produces higher returns, allowing carriers to use better interest rates at any given point of time.

Annuity payments and their terms are set when the contract is purchased; since the initial payment deferral date is often many years in the future, the carrier can make long-term plans to meet the expected payment obligations. The same yield curve explained in the "Variability" chapter applies here also.

The other DIA advantage is the mortality pooling. Normally, with regular SPIAs (initial payments starting within twelve months of the purchase date) mortality pooling starts after the initial payment date. However, with a DIA, mortality pooling starts after the purchase date. Since there could be a long deferral period prior to the initial payment, there can be a substantial deferral time between the purchase date and the first payment date. A cash value deferred annuity does not offer mortality pooling during the deferral period.

Of course, as we know from the "Variability" chapter, if the annuitant dies, then the joint annuitant (if there is one) or the beneficiary (if there is one) receives the remaining unpaid payments according to the terms of the SPIA.

DIAs treat annuitant death differently depending on whether the annuitant dies during the deferral period or after the initial payment commencement date. Typically, if annuitant death occurs during the deferral period and there is no joint annuitant, the entire contract premium and perhaps some interest is paid to the contract beneficiary. If there is a joint annuitant, then he or she takes over the contract as the new owner. Typically the joint annuitant is the spouse. If it is not the spouse, the contract might have special distribution rules.

Some DIA contracts do not have this death benefit provision and the contract simply terminates without value. In this case, the annual income is usually higher versus income from DIAs with a deferral period death benefit returning premium to the Beneficiary.

If the annuitant dies on or after the initial payment commencement date, the annuity payment terms are in force. Usually this does not translate to a lump-sum beneficiary payment.

The payment variability at the time of this writing is usually limited to interest and mortality pricing over one or two lives—meaning a single life with ten or more years period certain or a joint life with ten or more years period certain, etc. A few DIAs permit period-certain-only payments. These contracts have better legacy features, but because they don't incorporate mortality the payment pricing lags behind life contingent DIAs. Annual COLAs can also be found in some DIA contracts.

Deferred Income Annuity Uses

While modern-day financial planners are still finding ways to fully incorporate these reintroduced annuity contracts into their retirement planning models, I enjoy simple applications. By far the largest use of this contract is to augment age sixty-five retirement income. Another use that takes advantage of powerful mortality pooling pricing is to purchase the contract later in life, on or about age sixty or sixty-five, and start payments at or about age eighty or eighty-five. These types of DIAs may or may not feature a death benefit.

Defined Benefit Purchase Plan

Because many DIAs feature flexible premium designs, a person can purchase the contract in his or her forties and fund the contract with ongoing premiums over many years to grow the contract annual income. For example, a male age forty purchases a twenty-five-year DIA featuring an initial age sixty-five payment date for a ten years period certain and lifetime annuity. In this case, a $10,000 premium purchases a monthly income of $190 per month or $2,280 annually.

As the years go by, he can make annual contributions much like funding a defined benefit pension plan. But since this is a nonqualified deferred annuity, there are no funding rule limitations. Each time he makes a premium payment, he takes advantage of current pricing, so if pricing improves over the years he gets more annuity payment for his premium cost. Keep in mind as he ages, he gets closer to the initial payment date, usually fixed; given how interest compounds over time, there is less time between each new annual premium payment and the initial annuity payment date for interest to compound. Unless pricing changes and becomes more advantageous, each new equal premium will purchase less and less annuity payment. Some DIA contracts have features that permit the contract owner to change the initial payment date after the purchase date—to either escalate the date or further delay it. If the payment date is escalated, the annual income will reduce; if further deferred, the income will increase. These changes are usually limited to elections within five or ten years of the contract initial payment date.

Let's see what a typical premium purchase pattern might look like for a self-employed male, age fifty-five with an age sixty-five payment commencement date for a lifetime annuity with a cash refund feature. Each annual premium is $25,000.

DIA Consecutive Years Purchase Strategy

Age	$ Premium	Age 65 Monthly Income	Age 65 Annual Income	Non-Taxable Annual Portion*
55	$25,000	$228	$2,736	$1,185
56	$25,000	$215	$2,580	$1,174
57	$25,000	$203	$2,436	$1,172
58	$25,000	$193	$2,316	$1,179
59	$25,000	$183	$2,196	$1,184
60	$25,000	$174	$2,088	$1,188
61	$25,000	$161	$1,932	$1,159
62	$25,000	$152	$1,824	$1,156
63	$25,000	$149	$1,788	$1,194
64	$25,000	$143	$1,716	$1,199
Total	$250,000	$1,801	$21,612	$11,790

*The nontaxable portion is the premium cost recovery tax benefit over the Annuitant's lifetime permitted by the IRS for annuity contracts. Once the entire cost basis has been paid and the Annuitant continues to survive, the annuity payment becomes 100% taxable.

In this example, this businessperson pays a total premium cost of $250,000 over ten years and receives $1,801 per month or $21,612 in annual lifetime income; of this amount, $11,790 is not taxable. Because this contract has no cash value, this businessperson has to be comfortable with the fact he cannot access the contract values by making a withdrawal along the way. One feature is the contract premium payments are not a fixed liability. He can elect to not make ongoing payments or to pay different premium amounts. This is the flexibility of a nonqualified annuity. Of course, skipping payments or making payments in different amounts will affect the total annual income outcome.

However, once the premiums are paid, then the income purchase from that payment is guaranteed by the carrier. A male age fifty-five has a very good chance to survive to age sixty-five and begin to receive payments. Such an annuity could augment other savings, qualified plans, cash value life insurance, investments in real property or collectibles to fund his retirement. In fact, along with Social Security, another defined benefit plan arrangement; the annuity should be just one of many income sources. Because it is guaranteed by the carrier, if other retirement income sources don't pan out for various reasons—either bad financial markets or circumstances pertinent to the consumer—the annuity will be there to bail him out.

Because the payments are fixed after purchase, this type of annuity design allows a person to create a defined benefit target benefit or payment. Let's say the individual wants a total monthly benefit of $2,000. He or she just needs to manage to this purchase target amount. As the years go by, he or she can make premium purchases totaling $2,000 in annuity payments. In this manner the owner accumulates annual income. Typically, due to interest compounding from year to year and the mortality pricing benefit during the deferral period, the quicker the annuity is funded, the lower the ultimate total premium cost.

Alternatively, in our example, if this person had the available funds to make a single premium purchase at age fifty-five, his premium cost would be $199,136 to purchase the same annuity with a $1,801 monthly payment. But, because he purchases over a ten-year period in this example, it costs him $250,000 instead. If at age fifty-five this person started saving to purchase a refund annuity at age sixty-five for the $1,801 monthly payment, he would need to accumulate $350,957 to purchase this SPIA. This all assumes SPIA rates don't change over this ten-year period. Obviously the sooner you start, the less expensive it is.

As life changes, this person may get married and decide they want to make purchases with their new spouse. In this case, they can stop making payments into this contract and purchase a new contract with a joint and survivor annuity (see "Marital Property" chapter).

Advanced Life Delayed Annuity
"Advanced life delayed annuity (ALDA)" is a phrase coined by a noted industry actuary Moshe Milevsky in a study leading to a white paper published in 2004. These annuities are also referred to as DIAs.

The idea is to utilize the powerful mortality pricing that exists at older ages to supersize the annuity payment starting at age eighty to eighty-five when purchased by individuals age sixty to sixty-five. Because there is a good chance of death over this particular twenty- to twenty-five-year duration, the mortality element of the pricing is probably even better than the interest rate utilization. If the person survives to these advanced ages, they get a guaranteed annual income for a relatively low cost today. If the person doesn't survive to this time, typically the annuity terminates without value.

If you are trying to plan retirement with limited assets and you are age sixty-five, it helps to know you have to plan for a set duration of, say, twenty years to age eighty-five, when the annuity starts. However, if you go broke before age eighty-five, then you will just have to wait for your income to start—so if you and your planner use this strategy, don't go broke before age eighty-five.

Let's see just how much income you can purchase for a male age sixty-five with an age eighty-five annuity commencement date. Just a $25,000 premium purchases a lifetime annual income of $11,141. At this rate, the entire premium cost is paid in about twenty-seven months. However, because of IRS tables, the annual nontaxable amount is $3,621. At this rate, for income tax purposes, it will take 6.90 years to recover the premium cost. After this time, at about age ninety-two, the annuity income becomes 100 percent taxable. Of course, the annuitant needs to survive to that time.

While this looks good on paper, in real life these ALDA annuities are not widely popular. First of all, for a person who is already age sixty-five, a twenty-year deferral duration is quite the period indeed. There is a good chance many purchasing this contract will not receive a benefit because of death. Also, psychologically, it's difficult to get people to really worry about a possible event so far in the future; anything could happen over the next twenty years. These two issues don't typically compel individuals to purchase these kinds of DIAs.

By far, the widest use of these contracts is by individuals age forty to sixty and featuring initial payment commencement dates at roughly age sixty-five. First of all, there is a really good chance many of these individuals will survive to age sixty-five to begin receiving payments.

Second, these kinds of DIAs, like their SPIA brothers, are really safety mechanisms; while they will never make you rich, they keep you from going broke. Like I mentioned before, there are all kinds of ways to lose money, and DIAs are one of the best defensive financial products available in the market today. A DIA is only bested in this regard by the reversionary annuity.

DIAs in IRAs or Qualified Retirement Plans

New IRA and qualified retirement plan rules also incorporate DIAs. In a recent Treasury ruling dated July 1, 2014, such contracts may be purchased in IRAs or qualified retirement plans. These contracts are called qualifying longevity annuity contracts or (QLACs). Since these contracts have no December 31 cash balances on which to calculate normal RMD withdrawal calculations, the IRS imposes premium purchase maximums. The maximum QLAC premium purchase is the lessor of 25% of the retirement plan or IRA account balance or $125,000.

In other words, there are no RMD withdrawal requirements on premiums utilized to purchase QLACs in IRAs or qualified retirement plans. The later QLAC income, perhaps starting well after the maximum permitted age of seventy and a half for taking IRA and qualified plan income, produced by the QLAC will be the RMD income for that contract. The maximum age QLAC income can begin must be no later than the first day of the month next following the attainment of age eighty-five.

While other IRA income must start no later than April first following the year you obtain age seventy and a half, QLACs receive preferential treatment of continuing income deferrals up to age eight-five.

Reversionary Annuity (RA)

A reversionary annuity design has been around for many centuries. While it is primarily sold in Canada and the UK, there are a few US companies with a policy. If annuities are contracts, why do I say policy?

The reversionary annuity gets its name not for what it is, but for what it does. What it is; is life insurance, and what it does is pay a survivor lifetime annuity to the policy beneficiary when the insured dies. This surprisingly simple arrangement and benefit is an extremely cost efficient and effective way of transferring income wealth to a spouse or to the next generation.

Normally, traditional life insurance is used for this purpose, but there can be problems way after the life insurance policy is purchased that may cause the policy to lapse or be surrendered with little to no cash value. There also may be circumstances preventing the life insurance policy death benefit from being utilized for its intended purpose. These normal life insurance policy weaknesses are just the entrée for the reversionary annuity.

The reversionary annuity works by pooling mortality of not only the insured but also the beneficiary who receives the lifetime annuity. This mortality pooling method and survivor income–only death benefit allows the RA to pass much more estate value for its cost versus a traditional universal or whole life policy. You still need the lump-sum life insurance benefit to cover; final expenses, debts, college financing, charitable bequests and business transactions. However, as a strict income replacement mechanism for lost wages due to death, or Social Security or pension income, the reversionary annuity is unequalled.

Let's review the following case example.

In reality, an RA is a non-cash-value universal life (UL) product that creates a pricing advantage versus traditional universal life or whole life insurance by underwriting both the insured and the beneficiary for the monthly income (annuity) benefit/payment payable to the beneficiary when the insured dies.

If the beneficiary (irrevocable) predeceases the insured, the policy terminates without value. However, in this case, for an additional premium cost, the insured can be treated as a reversed beneficiary who collects a temporary life annuity upon the death of the beneficiary for the dollar amount of the premiums paid.

If the beneficiary dies first, the temporary life annuity is paid over at least ten years or 120 monthly payments. Under the terms of a temporary life annuity, the insured (now the reversed beneficiary) needs to live for 120 payments to collect all the paid premiums. The mortality trade-offs are what gives this design an income pop versus traditional life insurance when converted to income.

If you had a traditional life insurance policy and you died and the whole amount was converted to a lifetime annuity for your beneficiary, how much annual income will it produce? This is the sixty-four-dollar question all life insurance agents try to answer. Believe it or not, it's almost impossible to know! First of all, you have to make the assumption the life insurance policy is even in force at the time of death. But let's say it is—then you have to make a guess about what amount of annual lifetime income the life insurance can purchase when you go to convert the lump-sum death benefit to an annuity. Because annuity rates are changing all the time, this isn't possible to predict. The other problem is you don't know what age the policy beneficiary will be when the insured dies.

Life insurance agents in general make all kinds of estimates such as purchase life insurance in amounts of; three times annual income, five times annual income, ten times annual income or $1 million of life insurance for every $50,000 of lost wage income due to death, etc.

With a reversionary annuity, it is just so much easier. If you want to insure a $2,000 monthly wage loss, Social Security or pension benefit loss due to death, then you just purchase a reversionary annuity that will pay your beneficiary $2,000 per month. It's that simple.

But let's make some estimates based on a few control facts. You purchase a new traditional life insurance policy and these are the following facts: you're a male and your age is sixty-five and your spouse's age is sixty. Both of you have average health and the life insurance policy has a $250,000 death benefit, the lump sum amount paid to your beneficiary spouse when you die. This policy is a universal life policy design and the annual premium cost is $7,200. The caveat is as long as you pay this premium, you can keep the policy in force to age one hundred. If you don't pay the premium in any given year, you will most likely lapse the policy, losing the coverage and any residual value.

The following table indicates the amount of lifetime annuity income your beneficiary spouse can purchase if the entire $250,000 is utilized for such a transaction depending on when the insured spouse dies. Since we can't possibly know future annuity rates, I used the current rates at the time of writing.

Spousal Annuity Income

Male Age Date of Death	Female Age Beneficiary	Monthly Income Life-only	Non-Taxable Portion
65	60	$1,210	$ 860
75	70	$1,464	$1,392
80	75	$1,712	$1,666
85	80	$2,054	$2,054*
90	85	$2,559	$2,559**

*Female age 80 non-taxable income for 10.14 years then, 100% taxable if she survives.
** Female age 85 non-taxable income for 8.14 years then, 100% taxable if she survives.

Assuming current annuity rates at various dates of death, the amount of lifetime spousal annuity income grows over the years because the $250,000 death benefit is fixed and because the beneficiary spouse gets older and older at each assumed date of death. Therefore, the possible annuity income becomes greater and greater as they both age together.

Now let's look at the income death benefit of a reversionary annuity assuming the same facts. The reversionary annuity premium cost is the same—$7,200 per year. What will that get you?

Reversionary Annuity Income vs. Life Insurance

Male Age Date of Death	Female Age Beneficiary	RA Monthly Life-only Income Guaranteed	Non-Taxable Portion	Increased Income vs. Life Insurance
65	60	$2,656	$1,888	119.00%
75	70	$2,656	$2,362	81.42%
80	75	$2,656	$2,586	55.14%
85	80	$2,656	$2,656*	29.30%
90	85	$2,656	$2,656*	3.79%

Wow! For exactly the same $7,200 premium cost, look at the age sixty-five date of death when the beneficiary spouse is age sixty. If the insured spouse happens to die just after purchasing the reversionary annuity, the reversionary annuity produces a whopping 119 percent more guaranteed monthly beneficiary lifetime annuity income than the traditional universal life insurance policy.

In fact, on a guaranteed basis you would have to go way out past the insured spouse's age ninety before the life insurance would out produce the reversionary annuity as a guaranteed income provider.

However, there is always the chance the beneficiary spouse could predecease the insured spouse, causing the reversionary annuity to terminate without value. This supersized income benefit does not come without a potential cost. Like I always say, there is no free money out there.

In this case, let's just reduce the reversionary annuity income to account for the additional feature, in the event the beneficiary spouse dies first, the insured spouse gets all the paid premiums retuned to him in the form of his own annual annuity paid in equal payments over ten years. The caveat is he has to live all ten years to receive a return of his entire premium cost.

In this case, with this feature, how much is the beneficiary spouse's lifetime income?

Reversionary Annuity (return of premium) vs. Life Insurance Income

Male Age Date of Death	Female Age Beneficiary	RA Monthly Life-only Income Guaranteed	Non-Taxable Portion	Increased Income vs. Life Insurance
65	60	$2,274	$1,617	87.93%
75	70	$2,274	$2,022	55.32%
80	75	$2,274	$2,214	32.83%
85	80	$2,274	$2,274*	10.71%
90	85	$2,274	$2,274*	<11.14%>

Even with the insured spouse's return of premium feature, the reversionary annuity substantially out produces the life insurance policy's lifetime annuity income possibilities on a guaranteed basis. It's only at or just approaching the insured spouse's age ninety the traditional life insurance policy begins to make income sense.

Now that the reversionary annuity beneficiary income dominance is established, what else do you get? Previously I mentioned lapse. What happens if the traditional life insurance policy premiums are not paid? In this case, the traditional life insurance policy terminates with no value. To be fair, some universal life and whole life policies do have a cash surrender residual value the consumer could withdraw and then lapse the policy at that point. However, this example universal policy has an imbedded guarantee no matter what, as long as the premiums are paid, the carrier will not lapse the policy; with that no-lapse guarantee lasting to age one hundred. In exchange for this guarantee this universal life policy design typically, as the policy ages, has no meaningful cash value.

But what happens if the reversionary policy premiums are not paid and the policy lapses many years into the future? The reversionary annuity typically has a vesting schedule in case of lapse. As you pay the annual premiums, you gradually vest in the monthly beneficiary survivor lifetime annuity payment. Depending on this schedule—which considers the age of the insured when the reversionary annuity was purchased and for how many years the premium was paid—the beneficiary, in this example, becomes 25 percent vested in the survivor lifetime annuity payment after ten years, 50 percent vested after twenty years, and so on. If your reversionary is a ten year premium payment policy, you are 100% vested after ten years. Unlike the universal life insurance policy in this example, if you lapse the reversionary annuity, you can never forfeit your vested benefit. That's a big difference in beneficiary value retention.

Another reversionary annuity advantage is some beneficiaries might just be better off with a guaranteed lifetime annual income. After all, if the beneficiary blows the cash lump-sum death benefit of the life insurance policy (which, in the real world, is known to happen from time to time), they will always have the lifetime reversionary annuity income. The lifetime income gives the beneficiary an anti-dissipation benefit, and in the long run it may end up being the only thing keeping the beneficiary out of the poorhouse.

Now, you are going to always need some life insurance to take care of things requiring upfront cash at death, such as final expenses, college tuition costs, charitable bequests, business transition expenses, and taxes. If income is your primary goal, however, then you have to consider a reversionary annuity because it is actuarially designed to provide the biggest death benefit income for the buck.

What else do you get with a reversionary annuity that cash-value life insurances, such as universal life and also whole life, don't provide? Because of its actuarial design, there are some ancillary benefits. Unlike universal life or whole life insurance policies and annuity cash values, depending on the state, the reversionary annuity policy will not be included in the bankruptcy or Medicaid estates because the reversionary annuity has no cash value—only an expectation of a beneficiary lifetime future income paid upon the death of the insured, if the beneficiary lives.

Because the reversionary annuity has no cash surrender value, consumers going through a bankruptcy or Medicaid asset spend down will not have to terminate their reversionary annuity coverage to satisfy the state or other creditors. This is extremely important because if you ever get into one of these jams, the contract or some portion of the contract, due to the vesting feature, will be there for you even if you have to lapse the reversionary annuity because you can no longer afford the premium cost. This protection prevents your beneficiary from being left out in the cold and helps to insure your wealth transfer to them. Traditional life insurance and annuities, for that matter, do not enjoy such a benefit to the same degree. This is covered more in-depth in the "Protection" chapter, along with marital property impacts of reversionary annuity policies.

Chapter Summary

• Since 2008, deferred income annuities (DIAs) have become increasingly popular. The DIA's simple design, guaranteed contract elements, and lack of moving parts make it easier for consumers to understand versus modern deferred annuity contracts. Once issued, a DIA involves no ongoing management chores, and DIAs stay in force as permanent contracts. The DIA's lack of liquidity keeps consumers on track and prevents contract payments from becoming dissipated.

• DIA contracts are typically purchased by those between forty and fifty-five, with payments beginning at age sixty-five. In some cases, DIAs may be purchased between sixty and sixty-five, with payments beginning from ages eighty to eighty-five. The initial payment deferral period can be up to thirty years from the purchase date.

• DIA contracts have the same payment variability and income-exclusion-ratio tax treatment as SPIAs for their owners and beneficiaries. A classic use of a DIA is to accumulate retirement income by making premium payments to the contract over time. The earlier premiums are contributed and the greater the amounts, the bigger the total DIA income becomes. A qualified DIA, like a qualified SPIA, is subject to the usual IRS RMD rules.

• A reversionary annuity is a life insurance policy that pays lifetime income to the policy beneficiary when the insured dies. Because of the pricing interplay between the insured and the beneficiary, a reversionary annuity provides greater annual incomes to the beneficiary than traditional life insurance, given the same premium cost. Reversionary annuity beneficiary income is taxed using the SPIA exclusion-ratio treatment. Because the beneficiary lifetime income becomes vested over time, consumers can't lapse (or can only partially lapse) a reversionary annuity policy. Like SPIAs, the lack of a policy cash value makes reversionary annuity policies permanent financial products.

ANECDOTES

"It's not the events of our lives that shape us, but our beliefs as to what those events mean."
—*Tony Robbins, American life coach and self-help author*

Introduction
I believe one of the best ways to communicate the value of a thing is to tell a story about it. Through language and the written word, a visual pathway can be created to communicate wisdom and relevance. As previously stated in the "History" chapter, wisdom is not acquired like knowledge; it's gained through observation. Throughout this book, there is a peppering of SPIA stories used to make certain points. However, this chapter is exclusively centered on how SPIAs made people's lives better. SPIAs worked to protect their owners and beneficiaries, with protection extended over many decades of SPIA ownership.

Mom and Dad: Not Long for This World
Several years ago, an agent and social worker brought a case to my attention regarding a group of young parents about transitioning some of their wealth to their minor children. She mentioned this was a special group of parents who would enjoy some current income but were primarily interested in transferring their wealth. Now, transitioning wealth to children is a normal financial planning topic

request, so I was curious as to why an agent would think this was particularly special and what the involvement of social worker was all about.

You see, she explained; *these are mostly young, thirty- or forty somethings—single, unemployed moms, living in apartments with their minor children. They don't really have any assets beyond a small corporate retirement plan or an IRA. Almost all of them are recently divorced or separated, and many are bankrupt. They just need a little income now to help them get by and want to pass on the maximum amounts they can to their minor children. Their families are for the most part fractured, and family members could not be counted on to look out for the best financial interest of the kids who were the beneficiaries of their retirements plans when they would come into the assets, or what was left of the assets. Their fear was some of the families could become predatory. Oh, yeah; I forgot to mention all the group members are terminally ill and won't survive past twenty-four months.*

Now, I could see why the agent and social worker were having difficulty. Because of my background, my own wife was also terminally ill and we had minor children at the time, I was asked to put forward some ideas. It was a pretty tough case, one of the toughest, and it was very heart-breaking to know desperate individuals who were in such dire straits and who were not long for this world.

Even in the best of family situations, long before death occurs, terminal illness, like other physical disabilities, destroys marriages and creates financial hardships. When one spouse suffers a chronic illness or becomes disabled, incidents of divorce escalate 50 to 60 percent. Match this fact up with little or no health insurance coverage or health insurance that doesn't cover all the bills, and that's why people also go bankrupt. Job loss inevitability follows a chronic illness or disability. These parents were at the end of their ropes, but they wanted to protect their kids.

By nature, their retirement funds survived the bank-ruptcies, but plan balances were small due to the relative youth of their owners. Also, what was left was going to be dissipated in short order due to medical expenses. What could they do that would give them some income now and simultaneously protect their young children? SPIAs to the rescue!

Some of these parents purchased joint and survivor SPIAs with their minor children. They received some income immediately—in most cases not more than $200 to $250 per month, primarily because their plan balances were small and the average child, because of their current ages, was estimated to live an additional seventy or eighty years, assuming a normal life expectancy. The child inherited the entire payment upon the death of the parent. In this case, the carrier had to reduce the payment to the parent and the child to make sure funds were available to cover a potentially long payment duration linked to the child's lifetime expectations.

What's more, normally, a parent, due to IRS required minimum distribution rules (RMDs), can't pass 100 percent of the payment to a child (nonspouse). But the IRS has special provisions for SPIAs in this regard when the IRA owner—the parent, in this case—is substantially under age seventy at the time of SPIA purchase. For a SPIA agent, it's all about knowing the rules (see "Brokerage" chapter) and playing the game better than anyone else to obtain what your client needs.

While the parents received a little current income now, what did the kids get at their parents' deaths? They inherited, bypassing the probate process, an irrevocable income only paid to them if they survive. The income is only valuable to the child. While a court-appointed guardian would have to be appointed to direct the child's affairs until the child reached the age of majority (which in most states is age eighteen), the guardian would not be able to convert the future income to a lump sum. The guardian would be required by the court to spend the current income or save it for the benefit of their charge. Upon the death of the parent, the guardian would also have to contact the insurance company to update the income payment address with that of the minor child and execute a new election of tax withholding. Short of all this, the carrier will just withhold the payments until they can make sure the minor child is receiving them.

Even if the guardian attempted to hide the asset (SPIA) from the child, once the child reached working age and had to start filing federal and state income taxes, the taxing entity would start to inquire why the child, now an adult, was not reporting the SPIA income for income taxing purposes, causing the income to eventually be located and revert to the adult child.

What does the child get besides safety? The child gets quite the inheritance; really, from small acorns might oaks grow (guaranteed). Such is the case for long-term SPIA contracts. If the child lives eighty additional years after the parent's death, and the income payment is $200 per month, this amounts to $192,000 (80 x 12 x $200)—not bad for a $50,000 or so initial annuity premium from his or her parent.

The Sick Old Man
Another SPIA case I worked on had to do with several siblings who were attempting to provide care in varying degrees for their father, who was suffering from dementia. The problem was only the daughter lived nearby, while her

two brothers resided with their families out of state. Years ago, when the father had all his faculties and better health, he purchased SPIAs with each adult child, and all thought his assets were sufficient. Now, with the cost of care rapidly eroding his savings, the daughter began to despair. Providing the lion's share of her father's physical care and holding his power of attorney, she felt more entitled to his assets than her absentee brothers. She began to shift assets, stocks, bonds, and other investment portfolios to herself and changing the beneficiaries on her father's investments and other assets that couldn't be readily shifted in her favor. It all started so slowly, but as her father needed more and more of her time and care, it eventually escalated into an all-out financial grab-a-thon.

However, there were those pesky lifetime annuity contracts her father had bought for her brothers. While these lifetime annuities could not be converted to lump sums, they had remaining period-certain payments the brothers stood to inherit upon their father's death. She could not change the beneficiary to herself because I knew the family dynamic and had the presence of mind to advise the father to name each beneficiary as irrevocable.

The irrevocable beneficiary status had the effect of allowing each brother to control their individual contracts with the father without him sharing contract ownership. The father remained the sole contract owner, received the income, and paid the income taxes. Even though the sister had her father's power of attorney, she couldn't change the beneficiary on each contract without each individual brother's written permission. Their inheritance was preserved, as was the father's wish in the first place. His lifetime annuities protected his sons' inheritance from their dominating sister.

The Widow

As a young agent early in my SPIA career, I had the opportunity to visit with a recently widowed lady. Her husband of twenty years had passed away, and she was only in her early forties. She had one minor-age daughter. I worked with her and her father, who was in his seventies and lived several hundred miles away but was staying with her to clear up her financial affairs. Her father was a sophisticated investor and listened intently to all I had to say.

As has always been my custom, I started with the SPIA presentation. The father mentioned they interviewed several financial advisors, none of whom had mentioned a SPIA. But, to be fair, in the 1980s, most financial advisors were not trained regarding SPIAs. Of all the possible financial products, dollar for dollar, SPIAs also have a tendency to compensate the advisor the least, so naturally, advisors are not too excited about SPIA attributes. (This is still largely the case even today.)

I told the widow and her father SPIAs were thought by many financial advisors to be terrible investments. Of course, they are, because they are not investments at all; they are insurance contracts. It's like dismissing bank CDs by calling them terrible mutual funds. Just as it makes no sense to call a bank CD a terrible mutual fund, it doesn't make sense to call SPIAs a terrible investment.

Just because you spend money on something that has a financial context doesn't make it an investment. Not everything is an investment. It's just a convenient word many people use to lump all things financial together so they don't have to give the different financial items separate thoughts. It's just all an "investment" to them. Of course it is; what else could it be?

After my dissertation, the father's perspective started to form. I explained how SPIAs were guaranteed and how their design protected individuals from future unintended consequences of events not in their control—that the contract would survive the father, and when he wasn't around or perhaps was not healthy enough to help direct his daughter's financial affairs, the SPIA would be there. A SPIA often also survives the financial advisor. If the financial advisor dies, becomes sick, grows old, or retires, the contract still does its job. The ease of the way income is paid without the burden of money management is paramount.

They were both in agreement on purchasing a lifetime SPIA with some of the widow's life insurance proceeds. The rest of the life insurance money, IRAs/retirement plans, and other assets from her husband's estate were invested in a series of managed securities accounts such as mutual funds and savings accounts. Everyone went their way, and the years clicked by without incident—until, as fate would have it, life struck again with a vengeance.

Several years later, the father passed away. The daughter, now in her early twenties, was still living at home and began to insert herself more and more into her mother's financial affairs. The mother, now suffering from a chronic illness and unemployed, really needed her daughter's help and felt beholden to her. The mother's assets slowly became dissipated in favor of the daughter. I received numerous joint calls from them both inquiring about "redeeming" the SPIA. They always received the same answer—not possible, but they were welcome to try by contacting possible third-party purchasers they could research on their own. Of course, I knew no third party was going to purchase a SPIA payment that would die with the mother, particularly now that she was chronically ill.

Unsurprisingly, the mother continued to own the contract and collect the income.

While this family dynamic continued to shake out and negatively impact the mother, following a major natural catastrophe, she lost her house. Unbeknown to me, it had been mortgaged and the equity stripped. The house, now completely uninhabitable, had to be abandoned. Several years later, when the bank that owned the mortgage took over the house, she received a 1099 for taxable income attributable to the loan amount, which bankrupted her. Most people who have never lost a house in such a fashion don't realize debt relief is a taxable event to the debtor. When the bank writes off the loan and deducts it from its tax return as a loss, it becomes income to the debtor. I'm sure individuals who went through Hurricane Katrina in 2005 learned this lesson well. This tax trap has since been modified somewhat, and now determining whether you will be taxed depends on how your equity was spent.

In fact, after a bankruptcy court appearance, the only asset the widow retained, after all this time, was the lifetime SPIA. Imagine that! It was actually doing what it was supposed to do: protecting her from becoming indigent. That one contract and her Social Security payments were the only things keeping her from becoming completely dispossessed.

God's Will
Early in the wee hours on Martin Luther King Day in January 1994, the California Northridge Earthquake struck forcefully and in eighteen seconds instantaneously and forever impacted a million people. Living with my family just six miles from the earthquake's epicenter, it's hard to describe the impact of such an event; words barely do it justice.

After being jarred out of a peaceful sleep and tossed from the bed, many parents slashed the bottoms of their feet on broken bedroom mirror glass and other items racing to their kids' rooms. Like other parents of the time, we found our way to the upstairs kids' room blocked by the door; the door jambs had shifted, tweaking all the doors inside their frames and freezing them in place—including the front door to the house. Panicking parents broke into the bedrooms to extract panicking kids. After getting the kids and negotiated our way back down the staircase, which had been ripped from the supporting wall, we went out where the sliding glass door once stood and up and over the six-foot fence surrounding our patio. Of course, at 4:30 a.m. and with all the power knocked out, it was pitch black and cold, even for a California January. The night was punctuated by distant burning fires in all four directions, a sickening odor of natural gas from broken gas lines, and people's screams. It was like something from a movie, as people rushed to secure their families with blankets in ungaraged cars and trucks. No one dared start their cars to keep warm for fear of igniting the natural gas in the air. We had to wait for sunrise. As the morning wore on and daylight broke, inevitably the extent of the damage became evident, and neighbor helped neighbor.

Dawn revealed most of our possessions were gone. This included; our house, cars, a financial planning and tax preparation business with the entire capital investment started just sixteen days earlier on January first.

As bad as this moment was for a whole lot of people, it was nothing compared to the financial devastation that continued to span over many years. Once the initial shocked passed and all the TV cameras gone, people were left to fend for themselves with little to no initial government response.

While many people, including myself, had earthquake insurance, the carriers for the homeowners were nowhere to be found. You have to understand in circumstances of such widespread devastation, because insurance carrier resources are limited, there is a certain pecking order when it comes to claims settlement determined by the size of the premium payer.

The first in line is the federal government, followed by the state government and then the city and county. This initial group is then followed by all the Fortune 500 companies and smaller businesses. The individual homeowner is just about last on the list of claims for carrier adjuster resources. Keep this pecking order in mind if you ever find yourself in a major disaster. In fact, even though we were covered by a major A+ rated insurance company, we didn't see an adjuster until February of 1995, fourteen months later; by then, it was way too late for us. By that time, we were compelled to walk away from a home that couldn't be lived in; life had to go on.

By 1994, I had been an insurance agent for almost ten years and had lots of clients with immediate annuity contracts. I also had worked in the charitable gift annuity (CGA) world, raising money for a local charity. Abandoning my now-shattered fledging financial planning and tax preparation practice, I started a new career in the structured settlement industry as a litigation economist specializing in personal injury and marital property matters for divorcing couples. As can be expected in all major natural disasters, litigation went into high gear, and the divorce rate shot through the roof. My new employer and I were busy indeed. Over the next several years, I worked on more than three thousand divorce cases and brokered roughly forty structured settlement annuity contracts and other related annuities for personal injury matters. The pace was tremendous, sometimes reaching 125 divorces cases per month.

The divorce rate escalated with the bankruptcy rate. Chapter 7 bankrupts had to have their cases adjudicated by twelve additional bankruptcy referees sitting behind a semicircle of twelve eight-foot foldable serving tables in the county cafeteria Monday through Saturday because it could seat eight hundred people at a time. It was a complete zoo. Major creditors from all the credit card companies and banks had staffed cafeteria annex rooms in a vain hope to entice individuals to continue paying their debts. The parking was so bad people parked their cars up to a half mile away and resorted to lugging their financial records in airplane luggage with wheels. This pace continued for an entire year.

I saw a lot of good people, through no fault of their own, become completely dispossessed. Any financial assets were quick dissipated in an effort to remain afloat and avoid bankruptcy. This included stocks, bonds, mutual funds, savings accounts, cash value life insurance, deferred annuity contracts, kids' college savings funds, and retirement plans IRAs and 401(k)s. What the earthquake didn't take outright, the later divorce or loss of health due to stress and depression did.

However, as I saw how my own clients and those of many others via the litigation practice faired during this time, I slowly realized individuals escaping with some semblance of financial dignity were Social Security recipients, individuals with defined benefit pension plans, and, of course, SPIA owners. While the first two are a product of circumstance depending on your age and your employer, SPIA ownership is entirely an elective purchase. That's the key— "elective purchase." You have to own the insurance before you need it in order for the contract to work for you. The SPIA contracts continued to crank out sorely needed income. Deferred CGAs and deferred structures protected their owners' wealth simply because these owners got to retain their contracts.

The Drug Dealer's Family

One of my very good attorney clients was a general law practice attorney in South Central Los Angeles. Now, South Central Los Angeles, at least in 1994, was still suffering from the effects of the Rodney King Riots in 1992 and was not the best place to be or visit. By this time, I was becoming entrenched in my economic litigation and SPIA work.

I received a call at my office in West Los Angeles from this attorney about a probate case that came to him via the court system. He wanted me to come see him. I always dreaded this car ride out to his office with the bars on the window and the buzzer at the door. What a dump! As I nervously parked my car to the closest space to his office so that I could position myself to still view it from a window inside, I wondered what this was going to be all about.

It appeared a local drug dealer in the area was shot and killed, leaving behind a spouse and three minor children. Like most other people, he didn't have a will. When people die without a will in place, some assets don't avoid probate, such as real estate, stocks and bonds, mutual funds, leases, collectibles, gold and silver coins, cash in safety deposit boxes and under the bed, and so on. These and other assets fall into the probate estate, and the state—in this case, California—has rules regarding who benefits from the probate estate and to what degree. The probate court adjudicates these cases.

Some assets, such as life insurance, annuity contracts, bank accounts, and some security brokerage accounts, permit you to name beneficiaries who, if they were named, immediately inherit upon the presentation of a death certificate. The probate court has no power over these assets.

However, in this case, most of the drug dealer's assets were being adjudicated by the probate court. He had accumulated quite an amount of valuable financial and real property (real estate) assets. He also had a large savings account at a local community bank but failed to name an account beneficiary, so this savings account also fell into his probate estate

I met with the attorney and the mother along with a Spanish interpreter. The mother was a complete wreck and was very paranoid over the circumstance of her late husband's death. I asked no questions.

The probate judge was having a real problem with the asset allocation regarding the minor children's legal interest in the probate property under the law. The minor children were entitled to a financial interest in the probate estate, and because of unsavory family dynamics and the amount of money involved relative to the three minor children; there were real concerns for their financial well-being.

Many "family" members with questionable intentions were surfacing regarding the financial concerns of the kids. The mother, who had legal custody, was besieged and emotionally stressed to the max. I didn't speak Spanish, so I became stressed too. As I was dealing with a distraught mother and frantic interpreter, wondering just exactly what was being interpreted, I was looking out the window. What about my car—was it still there? Did it still have all four wheels? I was thinking *this annuity business is just crazy; who does this stuff besides me?*

While much of the kids' probate estate interests were being converted to cash by the judge, he was having all kinds of problems with possible trustee or guardian powers that could impact their long-term financial interests depending on what he decided to allow.

I proffered the following solution. The court would order the purchase of DIA contracts for the benefit of the children to be funded with premiums due each child from the probate estate. This way, the court would not have to fret over trustee or guardianship financial issues and powers because the carrier acts as the de facto trustee. The contracts are issued under the Uniform Transfer to Minors Act (UTMA), and each minor receives no payments until his or her legal age of eighteen in California. The contracts have no cash surrender value, and the payments are made to each child after obtaining age of majority (emancipation).

The idea is for the minor children to receive some funds at the legal age of eighteen, and then, as they age and gain the necessary maturity to direct their own financial affairs, they come into more and more of the funds from their father's probate estate. A smallish payment starts at age eighteen, doubles at age twenty-five, doubles again at age thirty, and doubles yet again at age thirty-five. The contract's beneficiary is the minor's estate until, starting at age eighteen; the child has an opportunity to name his or her own beneficiaries, in case they don't make it to collect all the payments.

This type of structure can be accomplished today by using retail commercial DIA contracts, but not via a single contract because of the annuity "substantially equal" payment doctrine discussed in the "Tax Implications" chapter. Because the doctrine is only applied to single, stand-alone contracts, these kinds of payment increases can be achieved by using multiple contracts that are issued simultaneously and combined to create the desired payment effect. This annuity brokerage transaction requires four contracts per child; since there were three children, it involved a total of twelve contracts and twelve applications. It was a lot of work!

The judge approved the annuity purchase, and DIA contracts were purchased. The carrier guaranteed the period-certain only payments and the eventual guardian, the mother, was constrained by the court to report any attempted disposition of the contracts prior to each child reaching age eighteen.

The titles of the contracts (ownership) were transferred initially from the mother as custodian under the UTMA to each child for his or her respective contracts once he or she reached age eighteen. While they remained minors, the non-cash-value aspect of the contract protected them and financially constrained the trustee or guardian. After the children assumed ownership, the escalating annual income allowed them to benefit from their father's estate gradually as they gained the necessary maturity to deal with their own financial affairs. As their own families changed, as the new owners they also had the opportunity to name their own contract beneficiaries and direct their payments. Once again, it was DIAs to the rescue!

The Wealthy Man's Eight Kids and Their Spouses
A wealthy widower facing family dissension over the eventual disposition of his rather large estate after his death—an estate that included significant real property and a family business—elected to help quell the family disturbance by establishing a crafty way of making most of the family happy.

Among the problems he faced was his own ill health, perceived to be additionally aggravated by family tensions; a current need for income with income tax advantages; the need for an agreeable family member to take over the reins should his health continue to fail or should he die; and a way to equalize the distribution of illiquid estate property among his eight children and their spouses and families. These were not easy tasks, considering the kids were already at each other's throats. What's more, after inheriting, some of the kids were going to be more successful than others in this regard, and all had long-term simmering sibling rivalry issues.

So often the success of any family wealth transfer is more predicated on those who receive it rather than those who give it. There are smart ways to transfer wealth, but a lot depends on the recipients. Parents have to be honest and really know their children. I often say a big wealth transfer is enabling. It makes it easier for individuals to become who they really are. Depending on the child, there are ways that are smarter to give and allow him or her to reap the long-term benefits you wish to confer.

While this was a complicated, multi-faceted case, most of it rested on control issues. Who was going to have the father's power of attorney, and who might be named his conservator depending on his deteriorating health situation? Which children would be comfortable with which siblings controlling the estate? It was difficult to measure which kids could successfully work together and be more comfortable running the family business and which kids would benefit more from the real property transfers at his death.

In these kinds of cases, life insurance can sometimes be used to help solve some of these issues. But the father, as many people do, waited too long, and now his advanced age and poor health circumstances negated the potential use of life insurance. He was fortunate, however, because he also had at his disposal significant cash and other near-cash assets, such as mutual funds, stocks, bonds, and so on.

SPIAs helped seal the deal. It was eventually determined he would purchase eight SPIA contracts, including himself and each one of his kids on separate contracts—placing, for example, Dad and the first child on the first contract, Dad and the second child on the second contract, and so on until all eight contracts were so disposed. The premium cost varied by contract depending on how much income he wished to confer on each child to help create an overall equitable distribution of his estate. Until he died, he collected all the contract income and paid all the income taxes associated with each contract—most of it not taxable due to the SPIA tax rules—and each child became a joint annuitant. Upon his death, each joint annuitant (child) inherited his or her respective income from Dad among all the remaining estate assets, according to his or her ability to manage each asset.

Most of the siblings were happy knowing at least some of their father's estate would automatically go to them immediately upon his death and in the interim period preceding his death, which might be affected by a chronic decline of heath, none of the siblings could interfere with the others' transfers.

There was no need to draw up complicated legal documents about what sibling-forced amalgamated committee might arise to manage the annuity portion of Dad's estate, either before or after his demise. These particular SPIA contracts worked magnificently to help him partition his estate in a reasonable and equitable manner depending on each child's abilities and allowed a passing of an equal and agreeable control to his tremendous brood of kids of his remaining assets.

What Might Have Been

While the above are great SPIA stories, I often think of what might have been had these simple contracts been in place for a host of individuals who were not so fortunate. Many of these stories are just heartbreaking and serve as excellent examples of the plight individuals can face when they don't have financial products like SPIAs and reversionary annuities to keep them from going broke and to protect their kids.

Financial Elder Abuse

The case with the most notoriety is that of Anthony D. Marshal and his elderly philanthropist mother, Brooke Astor. Millions were looted from Ms. Astor when Marshal and an attorney, Francis Morrissey, conspired to amend Ms. Astor's will in Marshal's favor. She was robbed blind while she fell into illness and became dispossessed. There was a trial, and both men received prison sentences they are appealing.

In another high-profile case, there was the battle between Anna Nicole Smith and E. Pierce Marshal over the estate of J. Howard Marshal II, an oil tycoon. In 1994, J. Howard Marshal II married Anna Nicole Smith when he was eighty-nine and she was twenty-six. J. Howard Marshal died in 1995, and Anna Nicole Smith spent the rest of her life fighting E. Pierce Marshal, her husband's son, over the disposition of his father's massive estate, estimated at about $1.6 billion with about $300 million contested. It was later determined E. Pierce Marshal undermined his late father's estate by destroying documents and stripping his father of assets prior to his father's death.

How much easier for Anna Nicole Smith would it have been if J Howard Marshal II had just purchased a joint and survivor with period-certain duration (as she was so young, this would have been a small extra cost) annuity with Anna Nicole Smith. He would have collected all the income, and then, at his death, all Anna Nicole Smith would have had to do is waltz into the insurance company home office with a death certificate. There wouldn't have been anything E. Pierce Marshal could have done about it. A $50 million annuity premium only represented a mere 3.1 percent of his net worth. In 1995, this lifetime annuity would have purchased an estimated $2.5 million per year for Anna Nicole Smith.

Looking at everyday cases, there was the case of Elsie Brooks. When Elsie was seventy-two, she sold her home and moved in with her daughter and granddaughter. Both assumed control of Elsie's accounts and proceeded to drain her finances, including a deferred annuity. They took her jewelry and furniture, and left her at a nursing facility. Both were convicted of grand theft and financial elder abuse. [2]

In another case, Rodeny Chapman was convicted of stealing over $300,000 from eighty-six-year-old Gwendolyn Swank by convincing her to pay phony protection money from drug dealing in her neighborhood.[3]

One of the fastest growing crimes is financial elder abuse. A stalling economy and a progressively aging population create incentives for an escalation of cases. In fact, a MetLife Mature Market Institute study claims such abuses amount to $2.9 billion per year. The primary culprits are

---

[2] "Protecting Mom and Dad's Money: What to Do When You Suspect Financial Abuse," http://www.consumerreports.org/cro/magazine/2013/01/protecting-mom-dad-s-money/index.htm, January 2013, accessed April 2014.

[3] Ibid.

family, friends, caregivers, and neighbors. In fact, of 107 cases in the study, the average loss amounted to $145,000.

A recent survey by Certified Financial Planners (CFPs) indicated senior financial fraud was rampant, with 56 percent of CFPs reporting they knew of elderly clients who were victims of financial abuse. In this group, the average loss was estimated at $140,500.

Law enforcement and social service providers report ever-increasing caseloads choking the courts, with more than 90 percent due to so-called trusted family members or other close relations. The older person is isolated and manipulated by intimidation and fear. Caregivers have lever- age, and the risk of being taken several times is reinforced by the fear of losing a caregiver.

There are all kinds of additional ways to help protect this fragile group, and certainly mortality-pooled SPIAs and reversionary annuities can play a huge part in providing the necessary financial protections. While current annuity monthly income can be manipulated, the base contract remains undisturbed to generate future guaranteed income.

American Greed
Dealing with an entirely different segment of society, those who are wealthy, in good health, and financially astute also show vulnerabilities. One of my favorite television shows is CNBC's *American Greed.* I selected two episodes from season six of this show regarding the stories of Allen Stanford, episode sixty seven and Nicholas Cosmo, epi- sode sixty.

Allen Stanford, labeled "The Dark Knight" by *American Greed*, was once one of America's wealthiest men and was listed in the 2008 edition of Forbes 400. His reported net worth was $2.2 billion dollars. He allegedly purchased an island for $63 million and owned private jets and yachts. Founding the Stanford Financial Group, he sold $ billions of fraudulent, insured certificates of deposit from a bank he established on the island of Antigua. In 2009, his financial empire came to an abrupt end when it was determined it was nothing more than just a Ponzi scheme. By the time this was discovered, however, more than $7 billion had been looted from more than twenty thousand investors, none of whom, at the date of this writing, have seen a single dime returned.

Sandra Dorrell, a wealthy investor, toured the Stanford Financial Group offices in Houston, Texas, and was extremely impressed. It had beautiful floors, well-appointed furnishings, and even a classic spiral staircase. Her broker was there and introduced her to the certificate of deposit. She lost $1.3 million when the company folded.

Cassie Wilkinson and her husband lost six figures to the scheming Stanford, who is now serving a 110-year federal prison sentence.

"The sentencing for crimes like this has become so big and so long that they're comparing it to economic homicide, and really, that's what it is," she said. "Someone murdered the life that I knew, that I worked hard for. We were not born with money; we earned every single penny."[4]

Nicholas Cosmo, through his company Agape World Inc., duped some four thousand investors out of their life savings via phony real estate bridge loans. He eventually received a twenty-five-year prison sentence when Agape World Inc. collapsed in 2009.

Hairdresser Ellen Gabriel is one victim who said Cosmo destroyed her life when he duped her into investing her

---

[4] "Allen Stanford: The Dark Knight," Season 6, Episode 67, http://www.cnbc.com/id/100196985, October 2012, accessed April 2014.

$130,000 life savings in his scam. "Retirement isn't even an option," said sixty-four-year-old Gabriel, who worked for thirty years to build a nest egg. "I do work seven days a week. I've worked holidays...I just go...I go, I do."[5]

Louis Piccoli, forty-eight, now has a home in foreclosure and wonders where his family and he will go. "You panic one day that, you know, the sheriff department's gonna come knock on the door," he said."[6]

Then there was the granddaddy of them all, Bernie Madoff. He received a 150-year prison sentence after his firm looted an estimated $65 billion from an estimated thirteen thousand victims. Many of these were the wealthiest and financially astute investors in the country—people like Fred Wilpon, the owner of the New York Mets baseball team; Steven Spielberg, the movie director; and Elie Wiesel, a Nobel Peace Prize laureate and holocaust survivor who had his entire charity looted of more than $15 million, while both he and his wife lost their entire life savings. The celebrity list of Madoff victims is notoriously long.

But there was also a group that wasn't so wealthy. For example, seventy-six-year-old Burt Goldstein and his wife, Ruth, were both financially devastated. His home in New York was sold at a loss to avoid foreclosure. He and his wife now live in one room at his daughter's house. He dropped his LTC insurance, gave up his car, and applied for food stamps. His life is a nightmare.[7]

Sixty-one-year-old widow Patty Brown, her brother, and her ninety-one-year-old mother all had their entire life savings with Bernie. All Patty's husband's life insurance money

---

[5] "The $400 Million Rip-Off," Season 6, Episode 60, http://www.cnbc.com/id/100001212, April 2012, accessed April 2014.

[6] Ibid.

[7] "Wiped Out by Madoff," http://www.money.cnn.com/galleries/2009/news/0906/gallery.madoff_victims/2.html, last modified June 6, 2009, accessed April 2014.

was lost, and she had to move her aged mother in with her. She is currently unemployed, unable to find a job.[8]

Then there was Joe and Linda Stewart. He is age 56 and has two teenage daughters. The entire $210,000 of his father's inheritance and other savings were lost. Before the collapse his account had $1.150 million. Joe had no knowledge of Bernie Madoff having made a direct investment in the Agile Funds which ended up as one of Bernie's "feeder" funds. He claims there is a strong possibility of bankruptcy in the near future and his kid's prospects are significantly diminished.[9]

While the very wealthy Madoff clients won't be eating cat food anytime soon, the average person on the street was hit really hard.

The wealthy and poor alike all had investments prior to meeting Bernie. These probably consisted of stocks and bonds, mutual funds, savings bonds, federal and state government securities, deferred annuity contracts, cash value life insurance, mortgage notes, cash in the bank, and so on. At some point, these holdings had to be liquidated in order to transfer the money to Bernie.

I often think how life might have been very different for these individuals caught up in these schemes, often through no fault of their own. What if all of them, just prior to meeting Bernie and his ilk, had mortality-pooled just a measly 15 to 20 percent of their net worth with SPIAs and reversionary annuity contracts? Because SPIAs and reversionary annuities are permanent financial products, there would have been no way to completely fund Bernie's

---

[8] "Wiped Out by Madoff," http://www.money.cnn.com/galleries/2009/news/0906/gallery.madoff_victims/3.html, last modified June 6, 2009, accessed April 2014

[9] "Wiped Out by Madoff," http://www.money.cnn.com/galleries/2009/news/0906/gallery.madoff_victims/4.html, last modified June 6, 2009, accessed April 2014

coffers and all of them would have retained enough wealth to keep from becoming destitute and losing their children's inheritances.

Mortality-pooled SPIAs and reversionary annuities are the key to coming back from a setback. They form a financial base on which to preserve some semblance of living and can provide a financial platform on which to rebuild.

I wonder, where in the heck where all the annuity agents? Did Burt Goldstein, Patty Brown, and Joe Stewart even know an agent? If they did know an agent, did that agent even bring up the safety advantages of morality pooling with SPIAs and reversionary annuity contracts? It's hard to know the answer to this particular question.

I've shared all these stories, nearly seven thousand words in this chapter alone—and I have others, by the way—regarding SPIAs and how they and reversionary annuities might have helped, and I have not made a single mention of lifetime income. This is because SPIAs are all about safety, safety—and did I also mention safety?

Is your story in here or some version of it? Some people ask me, "What if I purchase a SPIA and bad stuff doesn't happen to me? I wouldn't necessarily have needed a SPIA." This might be true, but what's the downside risk of purchasing the SPIA and not needing the protection? You collect $1,000 a month for life; that's the worst possible thing that can happen to you? It doesn't sound too bad to me.

Over my entire thirty-plus-year career in the annuity business, I have had the absolute honor of working with these very simple contracts and with individuals such as these. I have witnessed firsthand the immediate annuity staying power and the influence they exert on people's lives many years after they were applied for and issued by the carriers. They have saved many people's bacon. They really do what they were meant to do: keep people from going broke, allow them to pass on inheritances, and provide peace of mind. As for lifetime income, well—that's just a by-product.

Chapter Summary

• Regardless of economic class, education, or temperament, anyone can significantly benefit from mortality-pooled SPIAs and DIAs. Since these very simple contracts are primarily long-term safety mechanisms, consumers can benefit from their decades of protection.

• Life is full of ups and downs, and often the downs result from no fault of our own. You cannot control them; all you can do is to position yourself to mitigate their effects. SPIAs, DIAs, and RAs do just that.

• SPIA agents take the high ground and work to protect their clients from a host of seen and unseen financial adverse events that may develop over many years, gathering on the slopes below. The SPIA agent gets to put a stake through the heart of the bad guy coming up that hill.

REPOSE

**"An idea, like a ghost, must be spoken to
a little before it will explain itself."**
—*Charles Dickens, English writer and social critic*

Summary
SPIAs, which are more than a thousand years old, are ancient financial arrangements, elegant in their simplicity and timeless in their applications. Like onions, every time you peel off a layer, another reveals itself. National SPIA sales, while increasing at the fast annual rate versus other annuity contracts, still lag behind dollar sales of fixed deferred and variable annuity contracts. In 2013, LIMRA, an insurance trade organization, reported $8.3 billion of SPIAs and another $2.2 billion of DIAs were sold to consumers, an all-time high.

Guaranteed by legal reserve life insurance companies and regulated by the states, their mortality-pooled structures rise to a level of consumer protection not seen by any other financial product. Mortality pooling protects the wealth of individuals, spouses, and even entire families.

SPIAs are decidedly old-tech in the annuity world, but in a modern hi-tech deferred annuity world dominated by fifty to eighty-page contracts, convoluted terms and conditions, piles of unclear literature, and confusing secondary guarantees, SPIAs stand out as a shining example of what can be right in the financial world. Their 2014 return in force from 1930s – 1970s dominance upon the national scene, a return that will only grow over time, is probably the greatest comeback since Lazarus. As the public wakes up to the alien invasion destroying their finances and tossing the country into a long, hard financial recession we still have yet to come back from—including crushing body blows to careers, savings, home ownership, and retirement incomes—we must realize, like in the movie *Independence Day*, sometimes to beat the bad guys, you need to use a little Morse code.

The case for kingship in the income world is certainly apparent. Even so, no one financial product is the be-all and end-all among the plethora of available products. As with other financial products, SPIAs work best when employed in a concerted fashion with other strategies. While SPIAs maintain the protection edge other products lack, you are certainly not going to get rich by owning one.

However, when combined with their IRS tax-favored income status for all the parties involved—and, in many cases, their rich incomes relative to the cost of premiums—they are certainly a welcomed addition to income starved, distressed, and safety conscious consumers.

The average person in our society today seems to barely have a chance. The higher income produced by SPIA/DIA and RAs mortality pooling and the safety of the design formulated over a thousand years ago might just be what we need to get through these darkest of economic times.

"That's the idea; always keep your hands up."
—*Joe Gould (Paul Giamatti) from the
movie Cinderella Man (2005)*

ABOUT THE AUTHOR

**"If the writing is honest, it cannot be
separated from the man who wrote it."**
—Tennessee Williams, American playwright

Gary Mettler, CFP©, CEBS
"The Annuity Maestro"

Gary S. Mettler, CFP©, CEBS, has a thirty-year, eclectic annuity career that has earned him the informal but accurate title of "the annuity maestro." His experiences as an annuity agent included legal and actuarial training, commercial retail contracts, charitable gift contracts, structured settlements, home office annuity product design, and advanced annuity sales. As a litigation economist, he specialized in retirement plan valuation and rendered thousands of opinions regarding defined benefit and defined contribution retirement plans property matters for divorcing couples. He is an experienced trial expert witness.

As a nationally published author, Mettler's annuity articles have appeared in numerous periodicals including Benefits Quarterly, Senior Market Advisor, LifeHealthPro and Financial Planning. In addition, his white papers on SPIAs and RMDs, DIAs and SPIAs and marital property considerations, and temporary life annuity contracts serve as research references for other industry contributors.

Mettler began his formal education at the United States Military Academy at West Point and completed studying business economics at the University of California at Santa Barbara. After having suffered a total loss of all his possessions following the 1994 Northridge Earthquake in California and working with countless families in his litigation economic practice, he has seen people at their best and at their worst. The death of his spouse several years later, leaving minor children in his care, cemented his commitment to working with individuals and insurance products, such as annuities and life insurance that work to protect individuals and their families.

ACKNOWLEDGMENTS

I have had the great opportunity of working with some of the toughest bosses, brightest agents, smartest actuaries, passionate authors, and most inspired thought leaders the life insurance industry has ever produced. All of them, to some degree, contributed in their own ways to the writing of this book.

A Special thank you goes to my good friend and colleague, Donald C. Fleming for his editorial review skills. His help was deeply appreciated.